A Sufi Commentary on the Tao Te Ching

The Way and Its Virtue

by

Seyyed Hossein Nasr

A Sufi Commentary on the Tao Te Ching

The Way and Its Virtue

by

Lao Tzu

Translated from Chinese to English by
Toshihiko Izutsu and Seyyed Hossein Nasr

Persian Commentary by
Seyyed Hossein Nasr

Translated into English with annotations by
Mohammad H. Faghfoory

FONS VITAE

Published in 2025 by
Fons Vitae
49 Mockingbird Valley Drive
Louisville, KY 40207
http://www.fonsvitae.com

Library of Congress Control Number: 2025932826

ISBN 979-8896400-028

This book was typeset by Neville Blakemore, Jr.

Printed in Canada

Cover: The Great Mongol Shahnama. Nushirvan writing to the
Khaqan of Chin, Chester Beatty Library, Dublin, Ireland

With thanks to Professor Anne Betteridge
and Dr. Linda Komaroff, LACMA

The Prophet, upon him be peace, said,
"Seek knowledge, even unto China."

Contents

Translator's Introduction 11
Remarks on the Title of this Work 14
Introduction to the Persian Translation and Commentary 15

BOOK ONE

Chapter One 27
Chapter Two 30
Chapter Three 33
Chapter Four 35
Chapter Five 36
Chapter Six 38
Chapter Seven 39
Chapter Eight 41
Chapter Nine 44
Chapter Ten 46
Chapter Eleven 49
Chapter Twelve 50
Chapter Thirteen 52
Chapter Fourteen 54
Chapter Fifteen 57
Chapter Sixteen 60
Chapter Seventeen 63
Chapter Eighteen 65
Chapter Nineteen 66
Chapter Twenty 68
Chapter Twenty-One 71
Chapter Twenty-Two 73
Chapter Twenty-Three 76
Chapter Twenty-Four 78
Chapter Twenty-Five 80
Chapter Twenty-Six 83
Chapter Twenty-Seven 85
Chapter Twenty-Eight 87
Chapter Twenty-Nine 90
Chapter Thirty 92
Chapter Thirty-One 94
Chapter Thirty-Two 97

Chapter Thirty-Three 99
Chapter Thirty-Four 101
Chapter Thirty-Five 103
Chapter Thirty-Six 105
Chapter Thirty-Seven 107

BOOK TWO

Chapter Thirty-Eight 111
Chapter Thirty-Nine 114
Chapter Forty 117
Chapter Forty-One 118
Chapter Forty-Two 121
Chapter Forty-Three 123
Chapter Forty-Four 124
Chapter Forty-Five 126
Chapter Forty-Six 128
Chapter Forty-Seven 130
Chapter Forty-Eight 132
Chapter Forty-Nine 134
Chapter Fifty 136
Chapter Fifty-One 138
Chapter Fifty-Two 140
Chapter Fifty-Three 143
Chapter Fifty-Four 145
Chapter Fifty-Five 148
Chapter Fifty-Six 151
Chapter Fifty-Seven 153
Chapter Fifty-Eight 156
Chapter Fifty-Nine 159
Chapter Sixty 161
Chapter Sixty-One 162
Chapter Sixty-Two 164
Chapter Sixty-Three 166
Chapter Sixty-Four 169
Chapter Sixty-Five 174
Chapter Sixty-Six 176
Chapter Sixty-Seven 178
Chapter Sixty-Eight 180
Chapter Sixty-Nine 183
Chapter Seventy 185

Contents, *continued*

Chapter Seventy-One	187
Chapter Seventy-Two	188
Chapter Seventy-Three	190
Chapter Seventy-Four	192
Chapter Seventy-Five	194
Chapter Seventy-Six	196
Chapter Seventy-Seven	198
Chapter Seventy-Eight	200
Chapter Seventy-Nine	201
Chapter Eighty	203
Chapter Eighty-One	205

In the Name of God, the Most Merciful,
the Most Compassionate

Translator's Introduction

The present book introduces the sacred text of one of the most important non-Abrahamic traditions interpreted through the lens of a Muslim scholar accompanied by commentary and comparison with Persian poetry, mysticism, and philosophy from an Islamic perspective. With a few exceptions and until the publication of his Persian translation of the *Tao Te Ching* in Tehran in 1400/2021, Seyyed Hossein Nasr has written mostly on issues related to Islam and various aspects of Islamic civilization and the Islamic intellectual tradition.[1] This book is very different from his other writings.

In his introduction to the Persian edition of this book, Nasr mentions that he did not intend to undertake a systematic comparison of Islamic and Chinese philosophies, but rather to present in Persian some aspects of the truth of the *Tao Te Ching* in philosophical and gnostic language. His commentary, however, is more than a comparative study. Nasr highlights the similarities between the two traditions and in the most subtle and yet straightforward manner demonstrates the transcendent unity of religions. This is a message that reverberates through all his writings. He also demonstrates the universality of the truth, that all religions meet in the realm of meaning and speak of the same reality, and it is only in the domain of form that they differ. He uses references to Islamic sources and Persian poetry, making the book easily understandable to Persian and non-Persian readers alike who otherwise may not know much about Taoism.

Even though in recent years several Iranian scholars have

1. Two notable exceptions are *Knowledge and the Sacred*, Albany: State University of New York Press, 1989, and *Religion and the Order of Nature*, Oxford & New York: Oxford University Press, 1996.

translated the *Tao Te Ching* into Persian,[2] the publication of this book along with a commentary by a scholar of Nasr's caliber was an historical event in Iran for four reasons. The first is Dr. Nasr's authority as an internationally renowned thinker, theologian, and philosopher. The second is his extensive commentary on the original text of the *Tao Te Ching*, which has opened space for the comparative study of religions in academic as well as religious circles in Iran. The third reason is that the publication of this book may pave the way for serious interfaith dialogue in the Muslim world and between Islam and other traditions, an objective that Nasr has pursued throughout his scholarly life. Finally, the fourth reason pertains to the prevailing religious environment in Iran; in a socio-religious and cultural-political environment that is heavily dominated by exoteric Shi'ism, writing about a lesser-known non-Abrahamic tradition and highlighting its similarities with Islam demands a great deal of courage. Nasr has demonstrated such courage at a time in which an exclusivist reading of religion, especially by certain segments of the Shi'ite clergy, does not tolerate such discussions.

Translation of a text of this caliber in which three civilizations meet is not an easy task. Just as the original English translation of the *Tao Te Ching* presented here was the fruit of a collaboration between a Japanese and a Persian scholar, through Nasr's translation into Persian and his commentary, this book becomes the scene of an encounter between Islamic and Chinese religions and civilizations, and Persian culture where Quranic verses, verses of the *Tao Te Ching*, and both Persian Sufi poetry and prose stand side by side.

I would like to express my sincere thanks to Professor Seyyed Hossein Nasr for allowing me to undertake the translation of the commentary. I am eternally grateful for his guidance, support, and friendship that spans over four decades.

Special thanks are due to several friends and scholars who read the earlier draft of the manuscript and presented perceptive and constructive comments and suggestions. I am particularly indebted to Dr. Nicholas John Boylston of Harvard who devoted

2. Some examples of the many recent publications of the *Tao Te Ching* are translations by Farshīd Qahramānī, Nashr-i Muṣallā, Tehran, nd.; Amīr Ḥasan Qā'imī, Kūshān-Qā'imi, Tehran, 1379/2000; Ali Zāri'ī Sulaymānī, Tehran: 1400/2021; Muḥammad Jawād Gawharī, Tehran: n. d.; and Muḥammad Riḍā Changīz, Tehran, 1400/2021.

many hours, patiently reading the entire text and providing excellent comments and editorial suggestions. I am grateful to Ms. Jane Casewit for her extensive editorial work and corrections, and to Mr. Ishaaq Valodia for reading and editing the final copy and presenting editorial suggestions. I cannot thank these friends enough for their time and help during the preparation of this volume for publication. Their comments and help greatly improved the quality of this work. Needless to say, the responsibility for any errors or mistakes is solely my own.

Mohammad H. Faghfoory
September 25, 2024
Mehr 4, 1403
Rabiʻ al-Awwal 22, 1446

Remarks on the Title of this Work

by Seyyed Hossein Nasr

The title of this book, which is the most foundational source of the Taoist tradition and one of the best-known sacred texts of the religions of the world, has several meanings. Even though its title is usually translated as The Book of the Way and Its Virtues, it includes the word "Tao," which has no synonym in any other language. The Tao is not just the way to reach the Truth, it is also the Absolute Truth Itself, termed *al-Ḥaqq* in the Islamic tradition, meaning "the Real" or "the Divine Truth." At the same time, It is also the Way to attain perfection and to reach the Absolute Truth. Moreover, the Tao is the Principle of all things in the hierarchy of being, and that which determines the nature of all beings and the principles of their existence. The Tao is also the source of virtue and salvation. It has both ontological and ethical dimensions, and is both individual and social, human and cosmic, practical, theoretical and existential. For these reasons the term "Tao" is used in the Persian text and is not translated. The Tao is the guide that leads human beings to the highest plane of the Truth, which is nothing but the Tao Itself. Thus, the Tao is the fundamental key for understanding reality in all degrees of Its manifestation.

******

Introduction to the Persian Translation and Commentary

by Seyyed Hossein Nasr

O Lord of the two Easts and two Wests,[3]
Open unto us the Gates of Gnosis.

The book presented here, the *Tao Te Ching*, is the revealed book of Taoism and one of the best-known sacred texts in the world. The historical origin of this book is not known precisely, but most scholars believe that it emerged in the fifth or sixth century B.C.E. The text is in Classical Chinese and it is composed of two parts and eighty-one chapters. Most experts believe that changes were introduced into the text of the *Tao Te Ching* over the centuries, as is the case with the Gospels but is not the case for the Holy Quran, whose the text is fixed.

The title of this sacred text contains profound meanings. The *Tao Te Ching* can be translated as The Book of the Way and its Virtues, though the term "Way" is not a complete translation of the term "Tao." For this reason, in the translation and commentary the original Chinese term "Tao" has been kept. The Tao is both the Way to reach the Truth and the Divine Truth Itself in all Its aspects, from the Essence of the Truth to Its manifestations. The Tao is both the Principle of all beings in existence and is the Principle of proper action, including art, as well as being the root of all types of true knowledge. The Tao has neither a beginning nor an end. It is eternal, and at the same time It governs over the world of existence. It is Hidden yet It is Manifest, and whatever exists, exists by virtue of Its Presence.

While it may not be necessary to mention that the *Tao Te Ching* is the origin and the most important source of the Taoist tradition, it is necessary to note that there are other very important sources on Taoism, such as a collection named and authored by Chuang Tzu.[4] More-

---

3. A reference to Quran 55:17-18:
رَبُّ الْمَشْرِقَيْنِ وَرَبُّ الْمَغْرِبَيْنِ [فَبِأَيِّ آلاءِ رَبِّكُمَا تُكَذِّبَانِ]

4. "Zhuangzi (Chuang-Tzu, 369-298 B.C.E.) The Zhuangzi (also known as Chuang Tzu), named after 'Master Zhuang' was, along with the Laozi, one of the ear-

over, over the centuries, numerous books appeared in China that are closely connected to both the word "Tao" and Taoist philosophy, and which deal not only with religion and ethics but also with other issues, as is the case with the famous work *The Tao of Painting*.[5] In recent decades this has also become common in the West with the publication of significant works such as *The Tao of Physics*.[6]

As for Lao Tzu, even though he is known all over the world, his exact identity and biography is shrouded in mystery. There is a wide spectrum of opinions among scholars on this matter, from those who completely deny the existence of such a historical personality to those who believe he lived in the sixth century before Christ, about a century before Confucius, and those who argue that Lao Tzu appeared after him.

Although this author's opinion on this issue is not authoritative, my personal conclusion is that Lao Tzu was a historical person who lived several centuries before the birth of Christ, and also prior to Confucius, in southern China. In this regard I have followed the conclusions reached by Toshihiko Izutsu.

In any case, hundreds of millions of Chinese followers of the Taoist tradition have considered the *Tao Te Ching* the revealed book of their religion, a book that not only explains the philosophical and metaphysical principles of the realm of existence but also illuminates ethical and practical teachings on both the individual and societal levels.

In contrast to that which some observers claim, the *Tao Te Ching* is not a philosophical text even though it contains many philosophical teachings. Rather, it is the revealed book of one of the most important religions of the world. It is a short book but every sentence contains profound meaning. As for the length of its chapters, it is quite similar to

---

liest texts to contribute to the philosophy that has come to be known as Daojia, or school of the Way. According to traditional dating, Master Zhuang, to whom the first seven chapters of the text have traditionally been attributed, was an almost exact contemporary of the Confucian thinker Mencius, but we have no record of direct philosophical dialogue between them. The text is ranked among the greatest of literary and philosophical masterpieces that China has produced. Its style is complex – mythical, poetic, narrative, humorous, indirect, and polysemic." Steve Coutinho, *Internet Encyclopedia of Philosophy*, accessed June 25, 2023. See also James Hamilton Ware in *Encyclopedia Britannica*.

5. Mai-mai Sze, *The Tao of Painting: A Study of the Ritual Disposition of Chinese Painting. With a Translation of the Chieh Tzŭ Yüan Hua Chuan; Or, Mustard Seed Garden Manual of Painting, 1679-1701*, Routledge & K. Paul, 1957. This text is on the metaphysical, Taoist aspect of Chinese painting. Its purpose is to express human understanding of metaphysical forces in the form of painting of landscapes, bamboo, birds, and flowers.

6. Frithjof Capra, *The Tao of Physics*, 5th Edition, Shambala, Boston, 2013.

the final section (*juz'*) of the Quran, which is composed of short chapters (*sūrahs*). The style of the revealed book of Taoism is like certain other revealed books in the sense that it presents the greatest possible meaning in the fewest words. For this reason, many commentaries have been written on it over the centuries, in each of which effort has been made to elucidate the hidden meanings of the text.

The Taoist tradition is of course ancient, but it is not limited to the past. Today Taoism has hundreds of millions of followers in China and is also practiced in countries such as Malaysia, Singapore, and Indonesia where many people of Chinese descent live. Taoist temples that are still active centers of worship are scattered throughout East and Southeast Asia. In China, there are still prominent Taoist masters, most of whom live in remote regions, and there are many who believe that some of these masters have discovered the Taoist secrets of longevity and live for a remarkably long time. It seems that such people are more easily accessible in Taiwan than in China itself.

The current state of Taoism is a continuation of its ancient tradition, in which two distinct expressions of its teachings can be seen: one is the esoteric and philosophical dimension, which deals with the works of Chuang Tzu and other eminent Taoist sages, as well as Lao Tzu himself and the *Tao Te Ching*. The other current is the popular dimension of the tradition, which is often mixed with magic and the application of certain branches of the occult sciences.

The influence of the principles of the Taoist tradition is present in practically all of the cultural, artistic, and scientific domains of China, from the natural and cosmological sciences to painting, and from medicine to architecture. An examination of the history of science in China shows that most schools of thought were influenced by the Taoist philosophy of nature. The most important paintings of Chinese civilization such as the masterpieces of the era of the Sung dynasty[7] are themselves manifestations of Taoist philosophy without which they could not be imagined. Up until our own time Chinese medicine, including both acupuncture and herbal medicine, has been closely connected to Taoist principles, and many masters of Chinese medicine, which has now spread widely in the Western world, are also masters of Taoist philosophy. The spiritual and psychological principles of space, known as Feng Shui,[8] still remain in use in Chinese architecture and urban planning

7. 960 to 1126 C.E.

8. "Feng shui is a Chinese art which is based on the belief that the way you arrange things within a building, and within the rooms of that building, can affect

today and have even become popular in the United States. The application of the principles of the Taoist tradition in Chinese culture and civilization is remarkably broad, not only in the past but also in our own times.

The influence of Taoist thought and teachings is still visible today in the various cultural and religious domains of Korea, Japan, and even parts of Southeast Asia. Japanese Buddhist gnosis, known as "Zen,"[9] which has become so well-known in the contemporary world, is not only related to the esoteric school known as "Chan"[10] in Chinese Buddhism, but is also connected to the Taoist tradition. Indeed, there are few cultural phenomena in the Far East in which Taoist teachings are not in some way present, and at the heart of the presence of this tradition is to be found the *Tao Te Ching*. From traditional music and poetry to medicine and architecture the impact of Lao Tzu and his teachings in this part of the world is always to be found.

******

The story of how this book came to be written is a long one, but I con-

aspects of your life such as how happy and successful you are." *Webster's New World College Dictionary, 4th Edition,* 2010. See also the definition in *Collins English Dictionary, HarperCollins Publishers: London,* "The Chinese art of determining the most propitious design and placement of a grave, building, room, etc, so that the maximum harmony is achieved between the flow of chi of the environment and that of the user, believed to bring good fortune."

9. Japanese Zen Buddhist Philosophy: "Zen aims at the perfection of personhood. To this end, sitting meditation called "*za-zen*" is employed as a foundational method of *prāxis* across the different schools of this Buddha-Way – which is not an ideology, but a way of living. Through *za-zen* the Zen practitioner attempts to embody non-discriminatory wisdom *vis-à-vis* the meditational experience known as "*satori*" (enlightenment). A process of discovering wisdom culminates, among other things, in the experiential apprehension of the equality of all thing-events. The most distinguishing feature of this school of the Buddha-Way is its contention that wisdom, accompanied by compassion, is expressed in the everyday lifeworld when associating with one's self, other people, and nature." *Stanford Encyclopedia of Philosophy,* First published Wed June 28, 2006; substantive revision Wed July 31, 2019.

10. Chan Buddhism: "The Chan School (*Chan zong*) is an indigenous form of Chinese Buddhism that developed beginning in the sixth century C.E. and subsequently spread to the rest of East Asia (Japanese: Zen; Korean: Sôn; Vietnamese; Thiền). Although the Sinograph "chan" transliterates the Sanskrit *dhyāna* or "meditation," and *Chan zong* can thus be translated as the "Meditation School," Chan was not distinctive within Chinese Buddhism in its use of meditative techniques." *Stanford Encyclopedia of Philosophy*, First published Wed Apr 1, 2015; substantive revision Sat Mar 2, 2019

sider it necessary to briefly present it in this introduction. Many years before I was born, at the end of the government of Sun Yat-sen[11] and the beginning of the presidency of Chiang Kai-shek,[12] my uncle Seyyed Ali Nasr was Iran's ambassador in China and Japan. Upon his return to Iran, he brought a large number of invaluable works of Chinese art with him, and many of them were given to my father. As a result, I was familiar with Chinese art from a young age, and these works remained in our home until the Iranian revolution [1978-1979], when my house was plundered and many of these works were stolen or lost.

However, during my childhood there was no discussion in our home of Chinese philosophy. This was in contrast to Indian philosophy and culture, which had a lively presence in my childhood ambience, especially since during his visit to Iran [Rabindranath] Tagore[13] had been hosted by my father, and so stories about India were common in our home. Nevertheless, there was also an awareness of the great civilization of China in our home, though at that time I had never heard the

---

11. Dr. Sun Yat-sen (1866-1925) "The Chinese revolutionary and political leader often referred to as the 'father of modern China,' who played an instrumental role in the eventual collapse of the Qing Dynasty in 1911. He was the first provisional president when the Republic of China (ROC) that was founded in 1912, and later co-founded the Kuomintang (KMT) and served as its first leader. Sun Yat-sen was a unifying figure in post-Imperial China, and remains unique among twentieth century Chinese politicians for being widely revered in both Mainland China and in the Republic of China Taiwan." *New World Encyclopedia.*

12. Chiang Kai-shek (1887-1975) "Head of the Nationalist government in China (1928–49) and later in Taiwan (1949–75). After receiving military training in Tokyo, in 1918 he joined Sun Yat-sen, leader of the Nationalist Party. In the 1920s Chiang became commander in chief of the revolutionary army. In the 1930s he and Wang Jingwei vied for control of a new central government with its capital at Nanjing, fought against Japanese and the Communists. After the war China's civil war resumed, culminating in the Nationalists' flight to Taiwan in 1949, where Chiang ruled, supported by U.S. economic and military aid, until his death." *Encyclopedia Britannica.*

13. Rabindranath Tagore (1861-1941), born in Bengal, was the most eminent poet of India before partition. Gandhi, the political father of modern India, was his devoted friend (indeed, Tagore is the one who gave Gandhi his title "Mahatma," meaning "great soul"). Tagore was knighted by the ruling British Government in 1915, but within a few years he resigned the honor as a protest against British policies in India. With his English translations of some of his poems, he became rapidly known in the West. For the world, he became the voice of India's spiritual heritage, and for India, especially for Bengal, he became a great living institution. W.B. Yeats wrote the introduction to the English translation of the *Gitanjali*, which won the 1913 Nobel Prize. Tagore's poems have been beloved in India by persons ranging from the famed film director Satyajit Ray to Mahatma Gandhi, who – as he broke his courageous 1933 fast – asked that Tagore sing the Mahatma's favorite song (#39) from the *Gitanjali.*

names of Lao Tzu or the *Tao Te Ching*.

My acquaintance with this book and with Taoism began in my second year at MIT, that is in 1951 and 1952. During those years I was going through an intellectual and spiritual crisis that resulted in my rejection of modernity and my acceptance of the traditional worldview. This transformation coincided with my discovery of and daily access to Ananda Coomaraswamy's library, which was unparalleled with regard to the traditional thought of in eastern civilizations. It was there that I was introduced to the *Tao Te Ching*. I immediately fell in love with this book and began collecting the various English and French translations of it, until I developed a particular intimacy with it. This interest continued after my return to Iran in 1958.

In 1962, while I was a visiting professor at Harvard University, I was invited to deliver a lecture on Ṣadr al-Dīn Shīrāzī (Mullā Ṣadrā) at McGill University in Montreal. It was during this trip that I became acquainted with Toshihiko Izutsu,[14] who was then a professor at McGill. This meet-

14. Toshihiko Izutsu (1914–1993), who was rightly called "*The Genius that Bridged East and West*," was born in Tokyo. He received his early education under his father's guidance and who introduced him to Zen thought. Toshihiko started to practice zazen meditation at a young age. He studied at Keio University, where he later joined the university as a faculty member. An exceptional linguist, Izutsu is said to have mastered more than 30 languages including Russian, Greek, Hebrew, Arabic, Persian, Sanskrit, Pali, Chinese, Japanese, and Hindi. His academic interest and expertise spanned Islamic studies, Eastern thought, and mysticism.

In 1959, Izutsu started traveling abroad with a scholarship from the Rockefeller Foundation. He spent two years visiting Islamic research centers in Lebanon, Egypt, Germany, France, and Canada, among other places. In 1967, he began to participate in Eranos, an interdisciplinary conference dedicated to humanities and religious studies where he presented many lectures on Eastern philosophy and theology. His contributions to Eranos conferences earned him his reputation as an outstanding scholar.

In 1969, Izutsu retired from Keio University and accepted a professorial position at McGill University. When the Tehran Branch of McGill's Institute of Islamic Studies was established, upon the invitation of Seyyed Hossein Nasr – the founder and President of Iran's Royal Institute of Philosophy – he moved to Iran, and began to teach and conduct research there. He remained in Iran until the 1979 revolution.

Izutsu was, as Seyyed Hossein Nasr described, "the unparalleled Japanese Islamist and philosopher and a remarkable linguist." who made invaluable contributions to a wide range of academic disciplines that include philosophy, ethics, history, anthropology, archaeology, library sciences, sociology, psychology, and pedagogy. Until 1979 he wrote mostly and published in English. However, when he left Tehran, he devoted himself to writing in Japanese until his death in 1993 in Kamakura.

His most important works on Islamic thought include the best-known *Translation of the Qur'an* into Japanese, *Taoism and Sufism, Ethico-Religious Concepts in the Qur'an, God and*

ing resulted in a close friendship between us, and when I established the Imperial Academy of Philosophy in Tehran in 1971, I invited Izutsu to become a faculty member of the Academy. He accepted the invitation and would come to Tehran every year until the revolution. Both before he came to Iran and while he lived there, we would often discuss the *Tao Te Ching*, and he was well-aware of my interest in Lao-tzu's teachings and the sacred book of Taoism.

One day in the fall of 1971, when Izutsu had just returned to Tehran from Japan, I was sitting in the beautiful garden of the Academy reading when Izutsu arrived. After we exchanged greetings, he took a book out of his briefcase and said, "This is the original text of the *Tao Te Ching* in Chinese that was published recently. Let us translate it into Persian." I had read in a newspaper article that during archeological excavations in China a few months before that a large tomb of one of China's emperors had been discovered and hundreds of terracotta statues of the emperor's companions had been unearthed along with a copy of the *Tao Te Ching* from the fourth century B.C.E., making it the oldest extant copy of this work. Japanese scholars had gained access to that copy before their Chinese counterparts and had published it. It was a copy of that edition that Izutsu had brought with him to Tehran.

I took the book from Izutsu and examined its beautiful calligraphy for a while, before smiling and telling him that regrettably my knowledge of Chinese language was limited to a few ideograms. He replied, "That is not a problem. I will translate it into English, and then after making any corrections that you wish in terms of language and style, you can translate it into Persian. In the end I will compare your Persian translation with the Chinese text and make any necessary changes." I thought about it for a moment and then replied that despite my

---

Man in the Qur'an, Creation and the Timeless Order of Things, Toward a Philosophy of Zen Buddhism, and *Language and Magic: Studies in the Magical Function of Speech.*

Izutsu passed away on January 7, 1993. His rich library was entrusted to the Keio University Mita Media Center. It consisted of approximately 10,000 volumes of Japanese, Chinese, and Western-language books, including some 3,700 volumes in Arabic, as well as extremely valuable library materials such as 90 Iranian lithographic books rarely seen outside of Iran.

Information was adopted from Keio Times, May 28, 2021, and *The Philosophy of Seyyed Hossein Nasr*, The Library of Living Philosophers, Vol. XXVIII, ed. Lewis Edwin Hahn, Randall E. Auxier and Lucian Stone, 2001, pp. 52-55.

Atif Khalil, "Remembering Toshihiko Izutsu: Linguist, Islamicist, Philosopher," in *Islamic Thought and the Art of Translation: Texts and Studies in Honor of William C. Chittick and Sachiko Murata*, ed. Mohammed Rustom (Leiden: Brill, 2023), pp. 528-547.

busy schedule I would accept his suggestion given my great interest in the book. For the next three years, whenever Izutsu was in Tehran we would meet two or three times a week in my office at the Academy and work on the English translation of the *Tao Te Ching*, completing it a few years before the revolution and then reviewing the final text together.

At that time I mentioned to Izutsu that I hoped to write a Persian commentary to accompany the text and then publish it in Tehran, but this was postponed as a result of my many other responsibilities. Then the revolution occurred and Izutsu returned to Japan. A few years later the English translation of the book was published there with some modifications but without the slightest mention of our collaboration. The English and Persian translations were in my possession, and a particular series of events caused them to remain there.

At the beginning of 1979, a year before the revolution, a major exhibition of Islamic art to be held in Japan was being planned, which was to be inaugurated by Queen Farah and Prince Mikasa, the brother of the Emperor of Japan. In January of that year I was informed that since the Queen would not be able to attend the ceremony, I should attend the event. For this purpose I left Tehran, first for a short visit to London, planning to go to Tokyo afterward.

I had the habit of taking my scholarly work with me on long trips so that I could work on it on the airplane, in airports, or anywhere else I could have the chance to research or write. Since my destination on that trip was the Far East, I decided to bring the translation of the *Tao Te Ching* with me, and it was this decision that saved this book even though this trip did not end in Japan. If it were not for this decision, this book would have also been lost along with the two other books that I had completed and that were stolen when my personal library and office were raided during the revolution.

It took a while for my family and me to settle in America, and then the necessity of writing other books and articles took most of my time, so I set aside the *Tao Te Ching*. After two decades, which included the publication of numerous works, such as the text of the Gifford Lectures, which was published as *Knowledge and the Sacred*,[15] I began the extensive project of *The Study Quran*,[16] which took ten years to complete, and which is now being translated into Persian by Insha-Allah Rahmati. In the meantime some of my younger colleagues and students, especially Nariman Aavani, insisted that I complete the [Persian] translation of

15. *Knowledge and The Sacred*, op. cit.

16. *The Study Quran: A New Translation and Commentary*, New York: HarperOne, 2015.

and commentary on the *Tao Te Ching* and have it published. I accepted their suggestion, and after completing *The Study Quran*, I turned to complete this book. I am delighted that after nearly half a century it was finally published in Iran.[17]

The commentary presented in this book bears certain similarities with Izutsu's precious work *Sufism and Taoism*,[18] but at the same time is fundamentally different from it. Izutsu's objective was to compare Taoist philosophy with the metaphysics of Ibn Arabi, and in that work, he devoted many pages to analyzing the views of these two great sources of spiritual thought and then to comparing them. My objective, however, was not to undertake a systematic comparison of Islamic and Chinese philosophy, but rather to illuminate some of the truths of the *Tao Te Ching* in Persian philosophical and mystical terms. To attract the attention of Persian readers I have occasionally presented examples from Persian sources and especially poetry that demonstrate the proximity of certain Taoist and Islamic teachings.

In preparing the translation of and commentary on this text, I made use of a variety of sources that were available, though of course within the limits of my knowledge of various languages compared to a scholar like Izutsu. It is also necessary to add that I did not make use of other Persian translations of the *Tao Te Ching*, despite my respect for those scholars who have translated this text into Persian over the past few decades.

Finally, I would like to thank Ms. Katherine O'Brien for typing and preparing the English translation, and to Nariman Aavani for typing the Persian text of the translation and commentary. I would like to express my gratitude to both of them.

Wa ma tawfiqi illa bill'ah

بود نامم حسین و نصر باشم   خداوندا مرا منصور گردان

My name is Hossein, and I am Nasr   O God! Make me Victorious.[19]

******

17. *Tao-Te-Ching: Ṭarīq wa faḍā'il-i ān*, Intishārāt-i Eṭṭilā'āt, Tehran, 1400/2021.

18. Toshihiko Izutsu, *Sufism and Taoism: A Comparative Study of Key Philosophical Concepts*, First paperback Edition, University of California Press, Berkeley, 2016.

19. This is a translation of a poem that Nasr wrote at the end of his introduction. Having mentioned Hossein and Mansur, I guessed that he alluded to and connected with Hossein ibn Mansur al-Ḥallāj. When I asked him this question, he mentioned that he thought of al-Ḥallāj, but he was inspired by Shaykh Maḥmūd Shabistarī and his poem was an allusion to Shabistarī's poem in *Gulshan-i rāz*.

بنام خویش کردم ختم و پایان   الهی عاقبت محمود گردان

I completed this book under my name, Mahmud   O God! Make my end worthy of being praised.

BOOK ONE

Chapter One

The way of which one can speak as "way" is not the eternal Way (Tao);
The Name that can be named is not the eternal Name.
The Nameless is the beginning of Heaven and Earth;
While the named is the mother of the Ten Thousand Things.
In the state of eternal Non-Being we see the invisible depth of the Tao;
While in the state of Being, we see the determinations of the Tao.[20]
These two are originally the same;
But they are called differently as they reveal themselves.
In that particular dimension in which the two are the same, they are called mystery, the mystery of all mysteries, the gateway of all subtle things.

In the first verse of this discourse, the transcendence of the Tao is emphasized, and it is established that anything that can be spoken of is not the eternal Tao. This is because by speaking of the Tao one has placed a delimitation (*qayd*) on that which is transcendent, infinite and beyond definition and description. Therefore, any name that we assign to It is not the eternal Name, because by giving a name to that Absolute Reality we in fact delimit It. In its supreme meaning, the Tao is the Divine Reality, which has no name nor description.[21]

> O Thou who art beyond imagination, analogy, conjecture and fantasy
> and beyond everything said, we heard or read.
> The gathering has ended and life has come to an end,
> yet we still remain at the beginning of describing Thee.

20. Alternative (Izutsu): Maintaining oneself in the state of passionlessness (or desirelessness) one may see the unfathomable depth of the Tao; while maintaining oneself in the state of passionfulness (or desirefulness) one may see the infinite determinations of the Tao.

21. Sa'dī Shīrāzī, "*Kulliyāt, Risālah-yi chahārum*," edited by 'Abbās Iqbāl Āshtiyānī, Tehran, 1371/1992.

ای برتر از خیال و قیاس و گمان و وهم   وز هر چه گفته اند و شنیدیم و خوانده ایم
مجلس تمام گشت و به پایان رسید عمر   ما همچنان در اول وصف تو مانده‌ایم

It is one of the mysteries of existence that the Reality that has no name is at the same time the source of the entirety of the realm of existence, and it is "the Name" that in Chinese cosmology is called "the Mother of all the levels of Heaven and Earth." It is at this stage that name and determination appear, that is to say, the world of multiplicity, which in Chinese culture is called "the Ten Thousand Creatures."

These levels or gradations of the reality of the Tao can be compared with the long-standing classification of existence in Islamic philosophy, for there is a great deal of similarity between the two. In our own philosophy, one of the fundamental classifications of the levels of existence is as follows:

- existence conditioned by something (*wujūd bi sharṭ shay'*)
- negatively-conditioned existence (*wujūd bi sharṭ-i lā*)
- non-conditioned existence (*wujūd lā bi sharṭ*)
- the Absolute Unconditioned Being (*wujūd lā bi-sharṭ-i maqsamī*)

These gradations correspond perfectly to the gradations of reality of the Tao.

In Far Eastern philosophy, the term "Non-Being" does not denote non-existence in the ordinary sense of the term, but rather "beyond the act of existence." Non-Being is Reality before Its manifestation in existence.

> We and our beings are non-existent displaying existence,
> Thou art Absolute Being, appearing in the guise of the
> perishable.[22]

It is in that Non-Being, which is beyond existence, that one must seek the Infinite Reality of the Tao to which Lao Tzu alludes as the invisible world. This is beyond the ordinary meaning of "invisible world" (*'ālam-i ghayb*), which is contrasted with the visible world (*'ālam-i shahādat*). "The state of Being," by contrast, denotes the created world, in which whatever exists is of the endless determinations of the Tao.

The origin, manifestations and determinations [of the Tao] are in fact one single Reality, which appears in various forms and with various names as a result of determination. This verse of the *Tao Te*

22. Jalāl al-Dīn Rūmī, *Mathnawī*, I:602. Quoted in *Knowledge and the Sacred*, 314 and 330. Translation Seyyed Hossein Nasr.

ما عدم هاییم و هستی ها نما   تو وجود مطلقی فانی نما

Ching is a manner of expression of the Unity of Existence (*waḥdat al-wujūd*) of Sufism but in a different language. In that Absolute Reality, which is the Origin and which is one with Its manifestations, a great mystery is hidden, and for this reason it is called "mystery." It is the mystery that is the source of all mysteries and from which all beings of the higher realm originate. This can be compared to the Hidden Treasure (*kanz makhfī*) of the Sufis.[23]

******

23. An allusion to the well-known Hadīth Qudsī: "I was a hidden treasure and I loved to be known, so I created a creation, in order to be known."
كنت كنزاً مخفياً فأحببت أن أعرف فخلقت الخلق لكي أعرف

Chapter Two

Part I

The whole world recognizes that which is generally considered beautiful as the beautiful, and there arises ugliness.
The whole world recognizes that which is generally accepted as good, and there arises evil.

Some translators have translated this part as follows: "All people consider beautiful that which is usually considered to be beautiful, whereas it can only be seen as ugly. All people consider good that which is usually considered to be good, whereas it can be nothing but evil."

This verse alludes to the existence of opposites in the world of multiplicity. In this world, human beings usually comprehend facts and realities by comprehending their opposites. If there were no evil in this world, goodness could not be comprehended, and if there were no ugliness, beauty would not manifest, and even if goodness and beauty did manifest, they would not be comprehended as goodness and beauty.

The appearance of all things is through their opposite,
Except the Divine Truth, Who has no like and no opposite.[24]

Only the Tao is beyond name and description, which means precisely "the Divine Truth ... has no like and no opposite."

Part II

Thus, Being and Non-Being produce each other by their very opposition.
The difficult and the easy complement each other.
The long and the short appear in relation to each other.
The high and the low incline towards each other.
Tone and voice become distinguishable in relation to each other.

24. Maḥmūd Shabastarī, *The Rose Garden of Divine Mysteries*: Gulshan-i rāz, edition, translation and commentary Seyyed Hossein Nasr, SUNY Press, Albany, Forthcoming.
ظهور جمله اشیاء به ضد است ولی حق‌را نه مانند نه ند است

Before and after are established in relation to one another.
Therefore, the sage turns to the principle of non-action
and practices the teaching of no-words.

In this part, "being" does not denote Absolute Being, but rather existence. It inclines towards non-existence and non-existence returns to existence. That which is difficult is the complement of that which is easy. If there is no long, short will not exist and vice versa, and likewise for high and low. If a monotonous sound were to be constantly heard, it could not be comprehended. If there is nothing in front, being behind has no meaning, and again vice versa.

The last verse of this part contains one of the most important concepts of Chinese philosophy, that is: *wu wei*. It has been translated as "non-action"; that is to say, to carry out an act without the ordinary meaning of action, even though such a thing might appear to be impossible. It is only the sage who can resort to non-action, and as a result avoid words or delimitations, but rather practices the teaching of transcending them.

Attaining *wu wei* is not possible for everyone. One must be a sage to attain this spiritual station. Besides "Tao," there is perhaps no term as fundamental as *wu wei* for understanding Chinese philosophy.

Part III

The Ten Thousand Things arise around him, but he rejects none of them. He fosters them up; yet he claims no possession. He does great things but he does not boast of his own work. He accomplishes his task but does not stick to his own merit. He simply does not stick to his merit; thus his merit never deserts him.

The sage is as the center of the circle of existence around which everyone is gathered, and he accepts them as they are and does not reject them. Rather, the perfection of his being bestows perfection on them without his desiring to possess them. Since he is a sage, profound and great things issue from him, yet this never causes pride or arrogance in him. He considers his actions to be his duties, and even though his actions are accompanied by virtue, he never feels attachment to or possession of those virtues, of which he partakes. He is in a spiritual station about which it has been said:

> I am the slave of the will of the one who under the blue sky
> is free from anything that takes the color of attachment.[25]

Spiritual freedom is precisely this lack of attachment to other than God. It is for this very reason that a person with open horizons possesses virtue, and virtue is always with him and never leaves him; that is, the Tao is always with him.

******

25. Ḥāfiẓ Shīrāzī, *Dīwān*, ed. Muḥammad Qazwīnī and Qāsim Ghanī, Tehran, Zawār, 1320/1941, p. 27.

غلام همت آنم که زیر چرخ کبود   ز هر چه رنگ تعلق پذیرد آزاد است

Chapter Three

Part I

Not to honor the so-called wise-man will keep the people away from vain emulation.
Not to value goods which are hard to obtain will keep them away from committing theft.
Not to display what is desirable will keep them away from having an agitated mind.

In a society where wisdom is valued, not only will there be individuals who are truly sages, there will also be people who feign being sages. If they are respected, people will try to emulate them and will be misled. A lack of respect for them, however, saves people from pointlessly emulating them. Therefore, not showing respect for pretenders to wisdom is beneficial for society. Similarly, if value is not given to that which is hard to attain, the people would not try to obtain it by any means necessary or even resort to stealing. A thief tries to steal that which is difficult to obtain and hence is valuable. Finally, not boasting of possessing that which is attractive and desirable prevents people going after it, losing their serenity, and having agitated minds. Displaying what is desirable incites the desire to obtain it in others, and this takes away their peace of mind and concentration.

Part II

Therefore, in governing the people, the sage empties their minds of vanity but fills their stomachs, weakens their baseless ambitions but strengthens their bones.
He always keeps them innocent of unnecessary knowledge and free from immoderate desire.
It is in this way that he ensures that "knowers" never have a chance to interfere.
Thus if one governs the people by the principle of non-action, the whole world cannot but be well governed.

Even though discussion in this part is centered on the sage, what is intended is the sage who is also a ruler, who not only possesses wisdom but also possesses the authority and capability to conduct the affairs of society. Such a ruler who acts with wisdom endeavors to keep people away from such traits as arrogance and boasting of power and wealth. At the same time, he pays attention to their livelihoods and other needs, the most important of which is filling their stomachs. Such a ruler tries to protect his subjects from the blameworthy trait of ambition, which is one of the illnesses of all societies. He endeavors to "strengthen their bones," that is to say, to strengthen the foundation of their material lives.

Acquiring true knowledge to the extent possible is indeed necessary, and is a positive goal for everyone. However, attaining superficial knowledge, which is in fact really only information rather than true knowledge and results in pretention, is negative, and the wise ruler tries to keep people innocent of this and to save them from egoistic and immoderate inclinations. By doing this, he prevents individuals, who possess cleverness but do not act truthfully and in accordance with the Tao, from managing the affairs of society. If the ruler resorts to the principle of *wu wei* and rules in accordance with it, conflict, war and destructive behavior will disappear, and the affairs of the world will necessarily be conducted in consensus and in peace.

******

Chapter Four

The Way (Tao) is an empty vessel, but use will never fill It up.
Unfathomably deep, It is like the ancestor of the Ten Thousand Things.
It blunts the sharpness of things. It untangles the knots of things. It softens the glare of things. And It Itself remains concealed in the dust of things.
It is like a deep mass of water; yet It seems as if something were there.
I know not whose son It is,
Yet Its (primordial) Image was there prior even to the image of the (heavenly) Emperor.

In this chapter, Lao Tzu returns to the metaphysical principles discussed in Chapter One in summary fashion. The emptiness of the vessel of the Way alludes to the fact that in Its highest reality the Tao is beyond the act of existence. It is a non-existence that always is, and the gradations of existence never fill that emptiness. This is because It is unfathomably deep, yet at the same time It is like the ancestor or the origin and source of all existing things, which are referred to as the Ten Thousand Things.

In the abode of existence, everything is in its proper level of existence and cannot go beyond it, for the Tao does not allow the sharp edge of each thing to go beyond its own level. The Tao untangles the knots of all things; that is, having illuminated each thing in accordance with its own nature It frees it from ambiguity and agitation. The Tao prevents the glare, or ontological manifestation, of things to appear to be more than they are, while Itself remaining hidden behind the veil of the existence of all things.

After likening the Tao to an empty vessel, Lao Tzu describes It as a great mass of water. When this water is calm, it is as if there were something present in it, the identity of which is unknown. So he states that he does not know what its origin is or "whose son it is." Although It is eternal, Its form, which here means Its reality, existed even before the heavenly Emperor, who in Chinese philosophy corresponds to Adam, father of humanity, in the Abrahamic traditions.

Chapter Five

Part I

Heaven and Earth are without benevolence
and treat the Ten Thousand Things as if they were straw dogs.
The Sage is without benevolence
and he treats the people as if they were straw dogs.

"Heaven and Earth are without benevolence" is taken as a criticism of the Confucian tradition whereby the quality of benevolence, humaneness or *Jen,* is considered the highest virtue. The Taoist tradition, by contrast, does not have a homocentric view, but rather can be called Tao-centric. For this reason, It treats beings as if they are "straw dogs."

In Chinese philosophy and religions, "straw dogs" is an allusion to religious ceremonies in which straw dogs are made and are then treated with the utmost respect before the ceremony. However, once the ceremony is completed, they are thrown out such that passersby will trample them under their feet. The sage behaves in a similar manner and treats people like straw dogs. In other words, the sage is not concerned with virtue in its outward and social meaning, but rather with reality in the Taoist sense and the virtue of the Way, not merely outward, social or individual virtue. This section, therefore, must not be taken literally as signifying the denial of virtue, for the Tao Itself is the origin of virtues in Its deepest sense. To understand this section, it is necessary to understand the opposition of the perspectives of Confucianism and Taoism.

Part II

The space between Heaven and Earth is like a bellows.
It is empty without being exhausted.
The more it works, the more comes out.
Speaking much leads inevitably to exhaustion.
Better it is to hold fast to emptiness.

This part is a reference to the significance of the void and the emptiness of the space between Heaven and Earth, which is likened to the bellows of an ironsmith. It is the emptiness of the bellows that makes it a bellows, and it is because it is empty that it does not become exhausted from activity. On the contrary, being empty makes it all the more active and causes it to produce more. In light of this simile, there is a reminder that excessive and vain talk is like filling that void in the bellows, and it is this that leads to exhaustion. The result of this truth is that it is better to be silent as much as possible, since silence is precisely this emptiness within the domain of speech, and with silence something of that metaphysical void is manifested.

******

Chapter Six

The Spirit of the Valley never dies.
It is called the mysterious Female.
The gateway of the mysterious Female
It is called the Root of Heaven and Earth.
Barely visible, it continues to exist forever.
Unceasingly it works, yet never becomes exhausted.

"The Spirit of the Valley" in Chinese philosophy is a sacred being that is the archetype of the Way, and hence is eternal. For Lao Tzu the valley is an empty space, the entirety of which has been encompassed by the infinite creative power, of which water is the cosmological symbol.

It is from the Feminine Principle that all living beings are born, and this principle is called "mysterious," for not only does it possess mysterious creative power, but the very being of this Principle, much like the creative power of the "Breath of the Compassionate" (*nafas al-Raḥmān*) in Islamic philosophy, is a Divine Mystery and is not rationally comprehensible. This Principle is the root, gateway and source of existence of all beings, from Heaven to Earth. In the terminology of Muslim sages and gnostics, this Principle is the origin of the realm of existence of all other than God (*mā siwa'Llāh*).

This Principle belongs to the invisible world and is hardly observable because it is not apparent. Only sages can witness it with the eye of the heart (*chishm-i dil, 'ayn al-qalb*). The outward eye does not have the capacity to see it.

This Principle is constantly active, bestowing existence on beings. However, since Its power of activity is boundless, It never gets exhausted through creation and never ceases Its activity. This verse alludes to the fact that God's creative power is endless, and the Divine Name "Creator" (al-Khāliq) is always and unceasingly one of the Names of God.

******

Chapter Seven

Part I

Heaven and Earth are long enduring.
The reason why Heaven and Earth are enduring
Is that they do not strive to be alive.
Hence, they are able to be everlasting.

The ordinary life of a human being is on the earth, where he lives, and beneath heaven, where he passes his life; both of these are long enduring. What is meant by this verse, however, is not heaven and earth in the ordinary sense, but rather Heaven and Earth in the cosmological meaning alluded to before. This Heaven and Earth have an enduring existence beyond the upheavals of human life, human experiences of heaven and earth, and the passing of historical ages. The reason for this permanence is that Heaven and Earth do not struggle to endure, and it is this lack of effort or "non-action" that is the reason for their permanence. This verse is another expression of the important Taoist principle that, like water, one must seek the lowest place and avoid transgression and overstepping. The result of such an attitude is everlasting life and lack of attachment. In Islamic philosophy, this absence of action is termed "freedom from attachment," as Ḥāfiẓ declared:

> I am the slave of the will of the one who under the blue sky
> is free from anything that takes the color of attachment.[26]

Part II

Accordingly, the sage keeps himself in the rear,
And precisely because of that, he is in the front.
He puts his own self outside of consideration,
And precisely because of that, "his self" is preserved.
Is it not because he is self-less that he is able to bring his self to perfection?

26. Ḥāfiẓ, *Dīwān*, ibid.

For this reason, a sage is not someone who struggles to achieve superiority over others. Rather, in the endeavors of life his effort is centered on living in accordance with the Tao, while avoiding effort to acquire and to achieve superiority over others. For this reason, "he is in the front," since he avoids excess, lives in accordance with his true nature, and does not pretend to be what he is not. He who lives in harmony with his inner reality is in front of one who tries to be more than he is. Of course, this statement does not mean one should not struggle to improve and to attain virtue. If it were so, travelling on the Way (of the Tao) and living according to it would be meaningless.

A sage does not pay attention to his own soul (*nafs*), that is to say he does not spend his life nurturing his soul and fulfilling selfish desires and demands. Rather, by ignoring it, he prevents his soul from becoming strengthened and dominating over his inner reality. This results in his soul, to the extent that it is real, being protected and situated in its proper place within his being, rather than expanding and taking over his entire being.

The last verse of this chapter raises a question that contains within itself the key to the entire chapter. It is only through selflessness that one can bring about the perfection of one's soul, eliminate its limitations, and elevate it to higher stations of the soul in the universal meaning of the term; that is to lead it to transcend the stage of "the soul that commands evil" (*nafs i-ammārah*) until it reaches the station of the soul that has attained peace (*nafs-i muṭma'innah*), that is well-pleased (*nafs-i rāḍiyah*) and well-pleasing [to God] (*nafs-i marḍiyah*) as has been mentioned in the Quran and discussed in Sufism.[27]

******

27. Quran 89:27-30: "O thou soul at peace! Return unto thy Lord, content, contenting. Enter among My servants. Enter My Garden."
يا أَيَّتُهَا النَّفْسُ الْمُطْمَئِنَّةُ ارْجِعِي إِلَى رَبِّكِ رَاضِيَةً مَرْضِيَّةً فَادْخُلِي فِي عِبَادِي وَادْخُلِي جَنَّتِي

Chapter Eight

Part I

The highest good is like water.
Water benefits the Ten Thousand Things without contending with any thing
And it itself settles where none would like to be.
There, water comes close to the Way (Tao).

This part is to some extent a continuation of the previous section, as Lao Tzu returns to the symbolism of water, likening the highest good to it. But why water? Because water is beneficial for every living being, while it has no claim to being useful. Thus, the highest good is that man should do good without claiming it or expecting any reward. One should do a good deed, and as Saʿdī said, "throw it in the Tigris."[28]

If a human being is like water, he can benefit the Ten Thousand Things without seeking a high status for himself. Rather, he settles in a place that is of no interest to others. The sage does not seek to compete with others, but rather does good because the good is good in itself, and one should not expect reward for such deeds.

Despite this truth, there is great reward hidden in doing good without seeking reward, and that is finding proximity to the Tao. The reward for a good deed is the good deed itself and its effect on the human spirit, and this effect itself brings one close to the Tao.

Part II

In daily living it is important to be as low as the earth.
In the state of the mind it is important to be deep and tranquil.
In the act of giving it is important to act with benevolence.
In speech it is important to be truthful.
In ruling it is important that the state be maintained in perfect order.

28. Do a good deed and throw it in the Tigris River,
so that God will give it back to you in the desert.
تو نیکویی کن و در دجله انداز　　که ایزد در بیابانت دهد باز

In doing things it is important to be competent.
In action it is important to abide by timeliness.

This part is a series of pieces of ethical advice beginning with humility, for which the image of the dust under our feet is used. From a spiritual point of view, humility is the first virtue that must be acquired, not only occasionally but throughout daily life.

Man cannot avoid thought and intellectual activity of one form or another, but most often man's thoughts are shallow. Thus, one must make an effort to think profoundly and reach the depth of matters. Likewise, ordinary thinking is usually accompanied by a kind of excitement, haste, and agitation. One must avoid this manner of thinking and endeavor to attain tranquility of thought. For proper thinking, tranquility is essential, and in order to reach correct conclusions one must avoid agitation and excitement so that one may think and contemplate in peace.

In the domain of action, generosity and giving everything to others (whether spiritual or material) holds fundamental importance on the condition that such action be accompanied by good intention, as opposed to helping someone with the knowledge that such help with mislead him and make him less fortunate.

Honesty and right-thinking are at the heart of the ethical teachings of all revealed religions, and Taoism is no exception. Throughout the *Tao Te Ching*, Lao Tzu alludes to this fundamental truth in a variety of ways. As in Islam, in both Taoism and Confucianism there is much emphasis on the significance of this virtue.

In traditional societies, preserving social order in accordance with the philosophical and religious principles that govern society has always been considered the fundamental duty of government, and hence Lao Tzu emphasizes the importance of this. Obviously, if perfect order had always prevailed in traditional societies, such emphasis would not have been necessary. However, even in great traditional societies like China that enjoyed much religious, cultural, and ethnic homogeneity, there was nevertheless disorder, rebellion, and struggle between different groups, and that is the reason why the protection of peace and order as a duty of government has been emphasized so much.

Success in performing these duties is possible only through competence. Knowledge is of course necessary, but putting such knowledge into practice requires competence among the people who make up society.

Finally, Lao Tzu advises that precision is also necessary, since without precision nothing can be done correctly. In accomplishing each task there must be care and precision, taking all relevant factors into consideration and without working haphazardly.

Part III

If one is careful not to contend,
One will never go wrong.

Taoist philosophy discourages competitiveness, but this should not be mistaken for lack of effort. One must perform every task with precision, effort and in the best possible manner, not with the goal of competition, but rather for the sake of doing good and giving things their due. If one acts in this manner, he will remain immune from error, and this applies to all of the domains of action indicated above.

******

Chapter Nine

Rather than hold a vessel in the hands and fill it to the brim,
better to stop filling it halfway.
If in sharpening a sword one makes the blade too sharp,
it cannot hold long.
If a hall be filled with gold and jade,
there will be none to protect it.
If riches and honors induce one to be arrogant,
one would end up by falling into calamity.
The task accomplished, one should immediately retire.
That is the Way of Heaven.

This chapter returns to the topic of the importance of being empty, avoiding excess, and the necessity of leaving time and space free for all affairs. As such, it is better that a vessel be half-filled than full. This principle is applicable to human beings as well, meaning that for health it is better not to eat one's fill, but rather to stop eating while still feeling hungry, as is also the tradition of the Prophet of Islam.[29]

Likewise, the edge of a sword must be sufficiently sharp, but if sharpened too much, it will soon cease to function and will become dull. This rule also applies to precious things. Protecting a room that is empty or filled with things of low or no value is easy, but securing a room filled with gold and precious jewelry is much more difficult.

This truth can also be observed in man's inner and psychological life. If someone loses humility and becomes arrogant as a result of possessing riches and honors, the result for him will be nothing but turmoil and calamity.

The result of all these ethical truths is that man must not feel

---

29. Ḥadīth, *Sunan Ibn Mājah*, # 3349. "A human being fills no worse vessel than his stomach. It is sufficient for a human being to eat a few mouthfuls to keep his spine straight. But if he must (fill it), then one third of food, one third for drink and one third for air."

مَا مَلأَ آدَمِيٌّ وِعَاءً شَرًّا مِنْ بَطْنٍ حَسْبُ الآدَمِيِّ لُقَيْمَاتٌ يُقِمْنَ صُلْبَهُ فَإِنْ غَلَبَتِ الآدَمِيَّ نَفْسُهُ فَثُلُثٌ لِلطَّعَامِ وَثُلُثٌ لِلشَّرَابِ وَثُلُثٌ لِلنَّفَسِ

attached to the fruit of his labor or allow it to make him pompous, but rather must be detached. This manner of dealing with the affairs [of life] is the way to live in accordance with the Tao and to follow the Way of Heaven.

******

Chapter Ten

Part I

Controlling your vacillating bodily soul, can you closely embrace the One and never be separated from It?
Concentrating your breath and making your body supple, can you be like an infant?
Purifying your mysterious mirror, can you keep it spotless?
Loving the people and governing the state, can you keep yourself unknown?
As the gates of Heaven open and shut, can you keep to the role of the female?
Letting your illumination radiate to the four quarters, can you still remain in the state of un-knowing?

The teachings of this part are presented as a series of questions, each of which draws one's attention to an important matter regarding one's self. The first verse could have very well been said by a Muslim sage. To closely embrace the One is precisely "in God I trust" (*tawakkaltu 'ala'Llāh*) in the language of Chinese wisdom, and this is based on dominating the carnal soul. Never separating from the One is trusting Divine Unity, not only occasionally but consistently. Thus, the question is being asked, "O reader of this Heavenly Book, can you do this?" The same question can be posed to a Muslim, and the Noble Quran often presents the same question to believers.

Concentration on breathing and softening the body alludes to what can be termed a kind of Chinese Yoga, which is accompanied by reflection and contemplation in the spiritual sense of the term. These are actions that affect the body and the mind. Through such activities one can return to a state of child-like innocence, sinlessness and natural simplicity. Christ said that one must be like a little child to enter the kingdom of heaven,[30] and this corresponds to

30. "Truly, I tell you, unless you change and become like little children, you will never enter the Kingdom of heaven." *Matthew*, 18:3.

this verse of the *Tao Te Ching*, which is making this point in the form of a question.

The heart of man is a mysterious mirror, about which the Prophet said, "For everything there is a polish, and the polish of the heart is the remembrance of God (*dhikru'Llāh*)."[31] Polishing the heart removes the rust from it, and the heart becomes a mirror in which all of the realities of the spiritual world are manifested. So, if you polish your heart, you can preserve it in the same state and keep it from rusting again and losing its mirror-like quality. This statement alludes to the fact that not only must one polish one's heart, but one must also keep it polished and protected.

After discussing the inner life, this part turns to the outward world and relationships with others, once more emphasizing the Taoist virtue of remaining unknown and avoiding pretension. It asks, "Can you can extend friendship to others and even govern them without ostentation and pretension, that is, without this causing you to become arrogant?"

Sometimes one feels the blessing and grace of Heaven and at other times it is as though the gates of Heaven are closed. In such situations one must be patient and maintain receptivity and passivity, avoiding rebellion. So Lao Tzu asks if you can remain receptive and passive, which is referred to as the domain of the female, during this process of the opening and closing of the gates of Heaven. The Quran answers this teaching posed as a question when it commands, "Despair not of God's Mercy."[32]

One of the most significant obstacles of the spiritual life for those who aspire to spiritual perfection is involvement in disputation (*qīl-u qāl*), which should not be confused with the type of discussion that is important for acquiring formal knowledge. The more one becomes famous, the more important it is to avoid falling in the trap of disputation in spiritual matters, though not in the formal sciences. Thus, avoiding involvement in disputation in spiritual matters, the wisdom of faith (*ḥikmat-i īmānī*), and the

31. Ibn Ḥajar al-'Asqalānī, *Hidāyat al-Ruwāh ilā takhrīj aḥādīth al-maṣābīḥ wa'l-mishkāh*, 2226.

إن لكل شيء صقالة وإن صقالة القلوب ذكر الله.

32. Quran 39:53: Say, "O My servants who have been prodigal to the detriment of their own souls! Despair not of God's Mercy. Truly God forgives all sins. Truly He is the Forgiving, the Merciful."

قُلْ يَا عِبَادِيَ الَّذِينَ أَسْرَفُوا عَلَىٰ أَنفُسِهِمْ لَا تَقْنَطُوا مِن رَّحْمَةِ اللَّهِ ۚ إِنَّ اللَّهَ يَغْفِرُ الذُّنُوبَ جَمِيعًا ۚ إِنَّهُ هُوَ الْغَفُورُ الرَّحِيمُ

knowledge of certainty (*'ilm-i yaqīn*) is necessary for one who wants to reach to Tao and gain spiritual wisdom, and this becomes more difficult as fame increases. Thus, this verse is posing the question: "Now that you have achieved fame, are you able to remain immune from the pull of disputation and keep yourself above it?" The Sufis state that their aim is not to *qīl-u qāl* (disputation), but rather is *ḥāl* (spiritual states), as the following verse indicates:

The book of the Sufi is not the black ink of written words
It is none other than an unblemished heart like snow.[33]

Part II

The Way (Tao) gives birth to all things and rears them.
It gives birth to them, yet claims no possession.
It works, yet does not boast of Its own work.
It is the head of all things, yet exercises no authority.
Such is what I could call the mysterious Virtue.

In one sense, this part returns to the definition of the Tao and Its virtues. For this reason, the beginning of this part states that the Tao is the origin of the existence of all things, and It also nurtures and rears that which It has brought into existence. In other words, the Tao is both the principle of the existential origin of all things and the principle of their existential journey through the stages of becoming.

Lao Tzu then reiterates the importance of detachment and emphasizes that even though the Tao has brought all things into existence, It does not claim possession of them in the sense discussed previously. The Tao is present in all things and acts within them, yet never boasts at them nor feels proud of Its power and knowledge. The Tao is the head, which is to say, the principle of the existence of all things without using Its power of dominance in an anthropomorphic manner.

It is this wondrous truth that prompts Lao Tzu to call It "the mysterious Virtue." What could be more astonishing than the fact that the Tao is the principle of existence without exerting Its influence independent of the flow of existence and the essential nature of existing things?

33. Rumi, *Mathnawī*, II:159. Translation is taken from Seyyed Hossein Nasr, *The Garden of Truth*, New York: HarperOne, 2007, p. 58.

دفتر صوفی سواد وحرف نیست جز دل اسپید همچون برف نیست

Chapter Eleven

Thirty spokes unite in one hub.
Precisely in that empty space is the utility of the Wheel.
One kneads clay to make a vessel.
Precisely in that empty space within is the proper use of the vessel.
One cuts out doors and windows to make a house.
Precisely in that empty space within is the utility of the house.
Thus if Being profits us, it is due to the working of Non-Being.

In this chapter, Lao Tzu reiterates the fundamental importance of the void and Non-Being in the sense that was explained before. To explain this issue, this chapter begins with the example of a wheel, referring to the fact that many spokes come out of the rim of the wheel and come together at the hub of the wheel. However, what makes the wheel's action possible is not the spokes, but is more than anything, the empty space that connects them to the wheel.

Another example he uses is taken from pottery. While it is true that in order to make a vessel, we must first knead the clay and then shape a vessel out of it, what makes the vessel useful is not the clay, but is the empty space within it.

Through these examples, Lao Tzu concludes that if the existence of something is beneficial or useful for us, it is because of Non-Being and the void, or a certain mode of presence of the Reality beyond existence on the plane of determinations, which is to say the same Reality that is beyond existing things and is at the same time their source and origin.

******

Chapter Twelve

The five colors make man's eyes blind,
The five notes make man's ears deaf.
The five tastes make man's taste dull.
Racing and hunting drive man's mind into madness.
Precious objects hard to obtain serve to hinder his right conduct.
Hence the sage concentrates on the belly,
And does not care for the eye,
Therefore, he discards that and chooses this.

This chapter again discusses the effects of excess in every domain and the importance of attention to non-action and emptiness in the metaphysical sense. The external human senses are such that excessive use of them leads to their deterioration. For example, if the eye is exposed to extreme light, the result will be the loss of sight.

In ancient Chinese music there are five notes and nine octaves, and the above verse alludes to the fact that if one is excessive in listening to these notes, the faculty of hearing will become weak and one will eventually become deaf. Likewise, if one is excessive in tasting various foods, one may lose the ability to sense different tastes. What is meant by each of these examples is not to stop using these senses, but to avoid excess, in accordance with general Taoist principles.

Lao Tzu then presents other examples. Participating in horse racing or hunting, which create excitement and the pursuit of speed, removes man from his natural state and leads to an excitement that is a kind of madness. Similarly, going after precious objects that are hard to obtain prompts man to abandon right conduct and chose the wrong course.

Thus, the sage concentrates on his belly, which in Chinese medicine is the center of physical strength and spiritual power. That is, instead of paying attention to the outward senses and precious objects, he concentrates his attention on his vital and spiritual inner power.

Here, not caring for the eye signifies not caring for the external senses, that is, the sage has no interest in the pleasures that result from the external senses. Some commentators have suggested that it is possible that the belly alludes to the simple life free of luxury, and that the eye alludes to the life that is outwardly beautiful and to luxury adornments. Naturally, if this is the case, the sage concentrates on the belly and discards the eye, maintaining a simple life.

******

Chapter Thirteen

Favor and disgrace tend to upset man.
He tends to cherish great disaster as if it were his own body.
What is meant by saying that favor and disgrace tend to upset man?
Favor is (ordinarily) considered superior, while disgrace (is considered inferior).
This is what is meant by saying that favor and disgrace tend to upset man.[34]
What is meant by saying that man tends to cherish great disaster as if it were his own body?
The cause for my suffering great disaster is that I have a body.
When I no longer have a body what disaster shall I have?
Hence, he who values his body (in the true sense) more than dominion over an empire can be entrusted with ruling the empire.
He who loves his body (in the true sense) more than dominion over the empire can be given the custody of the empire.

If man is disgraced, he naturally becomes upset. But being favored can also lead to being upset because it renders one subject to jealousy and hostility. Being favored is usually not without difficulties even though it may initially make one happy. Moreover, favor may come to an end at any moment and cause one to be upset.

That which requires tolerating great difficulties to be obtained, such as honorable position, fame, or wealth, is also something to which man pays attention and loves in the same way that he is attached to his body.

Lao Tzu then asks, "What is the meaning of favor and disgrace such that they have the power to provoke man and take him out of his ordinary state?"

Being favored, like obtaining precious things or like grace and blessing, is naturally considered superior, whereas disfavor is considered inferior. For this reason, gaining positive things agitates man in its own way even though it temporarily makes him happy, and losing those things will also naturally upset and anger him.

34. Alternative (Izutsu): "In fact, favor is worse (than disgrace) for obtaining it one becomes upset and losing it one becomes also upset."

As to why man suffers as a result of great disasters, the answer is that he considers his physical body (as opposed to his subtle body) to be a real and valuable thing. If this is the case, and one does not possess a material body, what kind of disasters could descend upon him? Here "body (in the true sense)" alludes to one's inner self, and ultimately to the Divine Essence, which is hidden in the center of the being of everyone. If one values this reality more than dominion over an empire, it is only then that he is worthy of governing and is entrusted with ruling the empire, for he is no longer eager to gain power and impose his personal views on others.

Power is extremely attractive to ordinary human beings. Thus, only he who is aware of his inner reality, which is alluded to by the word "body" here, possesses the necessary qualifications to govern over others and can be called a righteous ruler. From ancient times and in various civilizations it has been said that, "He who governs over himself can govern the world."

******

Chapter Fourteen

Even if we try to see It, It cannot be seen.
In this respect It is called formless.
Even if we try to hear It, It cannot be heard.
In this respect It is called inaudible.
Even if we try to grasp It, It cannot be touched.
In this respect It is called subtle.
In these three qualities, It is totally unfathomable.
And so they merge into One.
In Its upper part It is not illumined;
In Its lower part It is not obscure.
Continuous interminably like a thread, It cannot be named.
It ultimately goes back to the original state of absolute indistinction (no thing).
(In reference to this point) should It be called a shapeless Shape or an imageless Image?
Should It be called (something) vague and undeterminable?
Facing It, we do not see Its front,
Following behind It, we do not see Its back.
Holding firm the reign of the eternal way of things,
It keeps in control the things of the present day.
It thus knows the primordial beginning of all things.
This is called the fundamental principle of Tao.

The subject of this chapter is the mysterious Reality of the Tao in Its fundamental principle and in relation to creation. As such, Lao Tzu declares that one can try to see this mysterious Reality, but this is a futile effort because this Reality cannot be seen.

Since what we are able to see is only the form of anything and we are unable to see its inner depths, it can be said that this Reality is formless. If It had a form, It could be seen. The same holds true for hearing. Only that which has sound can be heard. That Reality is silent and therefore is inaudible.

That mysterious Reality is not accessible, if by this we mean physically grasping It, for It is a Reality that is intangible; It cannot be perceived through sense of touch. Since It is intangible, It is called the subtle (*laṭīf*), not in the sense of being delicate, but rather in the philosophical sense of the term, as for example when the term "subtle body" is used, which means a body that exists on an existential level beyond that of the sensible world. Comprehending such a reality is only possible if one accepts the degrees of existence in the traditional sense.

Since this mysterious Reality is beyond being seen by the outward-seeing eye, heard by the corporeal ear, and touched by physical sense of touch, It possesses an endless depth that is unfathomable. It is this unfathomable depth that makes the three qualities mentioned above merge into one. If this were not the case, human consciousness would not possess unity and the various senses would have no relation to one another. It is this unfathomable depth that makes possible what the Islamic sages call "the common sense" (*ḥiss-i mushtarak*).

Lao Tzu then begins describing that mysterious Reality, presenting a description that is itself also mysterious. Contrary to what one might expect, he states that Its upper or higher part is not illumined. This statement is itself mysterious, for one usually associates higher realms with light and luminosity, and considers lower aspects of things to be accompanied by darkness. Lao Tzu, however, says that this is not the case.

Lao Tzu likens this mysterious Reality to a thread that has no end and therefore cannot be encompassed, or as he puts it, "It cannot be named." Ultimately, this mysterious Reality returns to Its original state, that is, "absolute indistinction." According to Muslim sages, Absolute Being is beyond all determinations, while all determinations issue from It and eventually return to this original state beyond determinations. In the arc of descent, creation issues from the undetermined Reality, and by traversing the arc of ascent returns to Its Origin beyond determinations.

After explaining these principles, Lao Tzu returns to a series of questions each of which contains a subtle philosophical point. He asks, can this mysterious Reality be considered "a shapeless Shape or an imageless Image?" Simply contemplating this question can lead to the ascent of thought beyond the material realm (*tajarrud-i fikr*) and the journey from outer form to inner meaning.

Lao Tzu then asks, "Should [this mysterious Reality] be called (something) vague and undeterminable?" Here vagueness does not refer to an intrinsic vagueness of this mysterious Reality but rather the vagueness of our apprehension of that Reality. A mysterious thing is not necessarily mysterious unto itself, but may only seem mysterious to the one who has not yet accessed genuine wisdom.

Lao Tzu returns to "describing" that mysterious and indescribable Reality using a series of apparently paradoxical statements. If we do not see Its front while facing It, what does it mean to be facing It? And if we cannot see Its front, what is it that we see that shows us that we are facing that Reality? Similarly, we do not see Its back, so how do we know that we are behind It?

These paradoxes lead to the assertion of fundamental truths regarding that mysterious Reality, the first of which is that It governs all things, much like the Divine ordinance (*mashiyyah*) in Islamic philosophy, which not only governs the present life but also the eternal journey of all things.

Likewise, the reign of [this mysterious Reality] is not only over the eternal way of things but It also "keeps in control the things of the present day" and of every day. As the Quran states, "He is Powerful over all things."[35] And since it is so, this mysterious Reality possesses knowledge of "the primordial beginning of all things" before their becoming, and not only the journey of beings in the world of becoming.

The conclusion of this discourse is that this mysterious Reality is the fundamental and foundational principle of the Tao, and it could also be said that It is the Tao Itself in one of the fundamental aspects of Its Reality. What is discussed throughout this chapter is in fact one fundamental aspect of the Tao, and the description found here can be considered to be very similar to the description of God in relation to His creation in Islamic philosophy and Sufism.

******

35. See for example, Quran 5:120:
لِلَّهِ مُلْكُ ٱلسَّمَـٰوَٰتِ وَٱلْأَرْضِ وَمَا فِيهِنَّ ۚ وَهُوَ عَلَىٰ كُلِّ شَىْءٍ قَدِيرٌۢ

Chapter Fifteen

Part I

From of old he who is perfect as a man is subtle and ungraspable,
his mind mysteriously pervading all things.
He is too profound to be known.
Because he cannot be known (as he really is), let me attempt to make
a forced description of the outward appearance of such a man.
Cautious, as if wading a river in winter,
Careful, as if in fear of his surroundings,
Formal and dignified as if on a visit as a guest,
Soft like ice thawing in spring,
Solid like the uncarved block of wood,
Vacant like a valley,
Murky like muddy water.

Attaining perfection is and has always been possible for every human being from the beginning of life in this world. Whoever achieves this perfection is subtle, in the sense that his spirit comprehends subtle realities and he is not limited to the material world and matters that pertain to the body and physical existence. As such, he cannot be comprehended using conventional criteria. His mind gains the power to pervade all things in a way that is mysterious and cannot be explained on the face of things.

"He is too profound to be known" by conventional criteria because the depth of his being is beyond comprehension and understanding through ordinary process. Lao Tzu adds that since this is the case he will attempt to describe the outward appearance of a person who has reached perfection, since this is indicative of his inner state. Of course, even when he speaks about outward appearance, it is not only an outward understanding that is being conveyed; rather, this description also contains inner meanings.

The one who has attained perfection is cautious in all affairs, like a man who walks on a frozen river during the winter. Before accomplishing any task, he considers all aspects of it "as if in fear of his surroundings," and, as we say, "He does not leap before he looks."

He is never heedless or excessively informal, but rather always behaves in a formal and dignified manner like a guest, which is to say, like a guest in traditional Chinese culture, not like a guest in the non-traditional world of today who might not necessarily observe traditional manners and etiquette.

The one who has attained perfection also avoids violence and one of his character traits is gentleness, which is likened here to "ice thawing in spring," which, in contrast to the ice of winter, is not hard and melts quickly. The one who has attained perfection is solid, that is, he is strong and stable in guarding his nature and character traits, like an untouched block of wood, which has not been carved or brought out of its original condition by any external factors.

The one possessing perfection is vacant, that is, he lacks delimitations and is in union with the void in the Taoist sense of the term, which here as on other occasions in this book is described as a valley. Finally, he is "murky like muddy water," meaning that his full depth and positive qualities are not visible to the eye that can only see the outward aspect of things.

Gaze upon the inner dimension of the world with the eye of inwardness,
For with outward eye thou shalt not see the inward.[36]

Part II

Who is there who is muddy and yet able to settle down
and slowly become limpid?
Who is there who is at rest and yet, stirring, slowly comes back to life?

This short section is comprised of two questions posed as riddles: First he asks, who is there who is muddy, in the sense alluded to in the first part of this chapter, but who can settle the mud of his existence, become fixed, and slowly become like limpid water? Second he asks, who is there who is at rest and yet, stirring, slowly comes back to life?

The answers to these questions are presented in the third part.

---

36. Nāṣir Khusraw, *Dīwān-i Ḥakīm Nāṣir Khusraw Qubādiyānī*, Edited by Karāmat Tofangdār, Tehran: 1374/1995, p. 66. Translated by Seyyed Hossein Nasr.
به چشم نهان بین نهان جهان را   که چشم عیان بین نبیند نهان را

Part III

He who holds fast to the Tao does not want to be filled up to the brim.
It is because he is not filled up to the brim that he (is like clothes that)
can be always worn and yet never in need of being remade.

In response to the questions raised above, Lao Tzu answers, "He who holds fast to the Tao." The result of this is that the vessel of his being is never filled to the brim, which is to say that there always remains an empty space in his being, which is precisely the space of the presence of the Tao. Since his being has this quality of emptiness, he is like a garment that can always be worn without it becoming ragged or needing to be remade. Making use of something that is corporeal results in its deterioration, but the reality of the spirit is another matter. However much it is used, it remains, and if it is used properly it is even strengthened. This also applies to the intellectual faculties, which are related to the realm of spirit.

******

Chapter Sixteen

Attaining to the utmost limit of emptiness, I firmly maintain myself
in the state of stillness.
The Ten Thousand Things all arise together, but as I watch them,
they return again to their Origin.
All things grow and flourish, but every one of them goes back to its Root.
Going back to one's Root is what I call stillness.
It means going back to the Command of Heaven.
Going back to the Command of Heaven is what I call the Unchanging.
To know the constant is what I call illumination.
If not knowing the constant one acts blindly, one necessarily falls
into calamity.
He who knows the constant is all-embracing.
Being all-embracing, he is impartial.
Being impartial, he is kingly.
Being kingly, he is in accord with Heaven.
Being in accord with Heaven, he is at one with Tao.
Being at one with the Tao, he is eternal.
His body may come to an end, but he never perishes.

Attaining the utmost limit of emptiness of oneself means gaining access to the presence of the Tao. That which is emptied of itself is filled by the presence of the Tao, and in Chinese philosophy this "being filled" is precisely that of being empty. At the same time, attaining this spiritual station requires staying firm in it, and therefore Lao Tzu says, "I maintain myself in the state of stillness." This requires a great deal of effort. Thus, one must firmly maintain oneself in that state.

The second verse describes contemplation of the created world from the perspective of the state of stillness. In this state, even though the Ten Thousand Things are constantly arising, from the perspective of the sage who is in the state of stillness, everything is seen to return to its origin. The spiritual man knows that,

> *Whoever becomes distanced from his roots*
> *seeks to return to the days of his union.*[37]

This reality is not only true of human beings but of all beings, as it is said, "All things return to their Origin."[38]

The third verse also repeats this truth in a different language; all existents grow and flourish, and ultimately return to their Root, which means precisely their Origin. This return is the same as returning to stillness. In the terminology of Islamic philosophy, becoming (*ṣayrūrah*) issues from Unchanging Being (*wujūd lā yataghayyar*) and again returns to It.

Lao Tzu calls this stillness "the Command of Heaven," which in Chinese philosophy can be interpreted as the Origin and Principle. The Command of Heaven does not change, therefore he calls the return to it "the Unchanging."

The return to the Command of Heaven is one thing and knowledge of it, though related to it, is something else. This knowledge is not rational knowledge but illumination. It is through intuition and illumination, not through discursive argumentation and the particular intellect (*'aql-i juz'ī*), that such knowledge is acquired. Only a sage possesses this knowledge and acts in accordance with it. However, if one lacks such knowledge and acts blindly, the consequence of his action will not be positive and will cause him to fall into calamity.

He who acquires knowledge of the unchanging Truth, the Tao, has in fact attained knowledge of the Principle of all things. Thus, one can say that his knowledge and his being embrace all things. Since he embraces all things, he looks at all things with total objectivity, and not from a particular point of view.

A person who possesses such total objectivity and remains impartial in all affairs is kingly. Since he is in this station, he is always in accord with Heaven, that is, with the celestial reality of all things. Since he is in harmony with Heaven, he is at one with the Tao, for it is the Tao that is the source of that harmony, or, rather, is that very harmony itself.

Being at one with the Tao is to attain the station of being eternal. Whoever attains the world of the Spirit and God has been de-

37. Rumi, *Mathnawī*, I:4. Translated by Seyyed Hossein Nasr.
هر کسی کو دور ماند از اصل خویش   باز جوید روزگار وصل خویش

38. Junayd
کُلّ شیءٍ یَرجعُ الی اصلِهِ

livered from the danger of perishing and gains eternal life. The human body is of course perishable, but such an individual who has attained union with the Truth is liberated from non-existence and his being will never cease.

******

Chapter Seventeen

The highest of all types of rulers is such that those who are under his rule are only aware of his presence.
Next is the ruler to whom they feel attached and whom they praise.
Next is one whom they fear.
Next is one whom they despise.
If (the ruler) is not trusted enough, it is because he is not truthful enough.
If the ruler be calm and composed, and utter (only) weighty words, then his task will be accomplished and his work done; and the people will say, "Everything that we have done, we have done naturally, by ourselves."

In this chapter, Lao Tzu returns to the discussion of characteristics of a ruler from the point of view of traditional Chinese philosophy, beginning with the highest and most exalted type of ruler. This ruler is one of whose presence the people are aware, even though he does not constantly interfere in their affairs. He is like a lamp, the very existence of which casts light on its surroundings without intervening practically in them.

Below that is the ruler who rules with justice and fairness, and as a result the people consider him as one of themselves and praise him. Next is the ruler who rules over people by spreading fear, such that the people obey his commands and submit to his rule not because they admire him, but because they are afraid of him. The worst kind of ruler is one whom the people despise and for whom they have no respect.

It is necessary that people trust their ruler and their government, and the fact of the matter is that the people want to have this trust, and if there is no possibility of such trust then everyone will suffer as a result. Lack of trust is the result of the dishonesty of the ruling class more than any other factor. This principle is not limited to China, and has always been observable everywhere and in every period of history, including the contemporary world.

By contrast, if a ruler is calm and composed, possesses the dignity of a sage-ruler, and speaks meaningfully and eloquently to his people, he will accomplish his task as a just and good-natured ruler. He will act in such a way that people accomplish their affairs correctly and will suppose that it is they themselves who have accomplished these things naturally, and not as a result of force and pressure from the government.

******

Chapter Eighteen

It is only when the great Tao falls into decline that virtues such as benevolence and righteousness become conspicuous.
It is only when cleverness and sagacity make their appearance that wiles and intrigues arise.
It is only when the six family relations lose their harmony that filial sons make their appearance.
It is only when the state falls into confusion and disorder that there are loyal subjects.

Benevolence and righteousness become apparent when there is a contrast arising from the duality of right and wrong, good and evil, whereas the Origin is beyond any kind of duality. Thus, it is only through the weakening of the Tao in its highest degree that this duality arises.

The subsequent verses of this chapter discuss the appearance of this duality in other domains of life. As such, Lao Tzu states that it is only with the appearance of cleverness and sagacity that their contraries – evil, ugliness and deception – also become possible.

The six family relationships in Chinese culture consist of father-son, older brother-younger brother, and husband-wife. If harmony between them declines or disappears, then filial sons will emerge, for if unfilial children did not exist, there would be no distinguishing feature by which a filial child would stand out among children.

Similarly on the societal level, it is only when a government declines and finally collapses that individuals who are loyal will be seen. If there were a government that enjoyed the loyalty of every citizen, the quality of loyalty would not be recognized in a distinct way. All these cases are in fact elaboration of this verse of Shabastarī's *Gulshan-i rāz*,[39] "The appearance of all things is through their opposite, except the Divine Truth (the great Tao), Who has no like and no opposite."

******

39. Maḥmūd Shabastarī, op. cit.

Chapter Nineteen

If (the ruler) abolishes cleverness and abandons sagacity, the people will benefit therefrom a hundredfold.
If he abolishes benevolence and abandons righteousness, the people will (spontaneously) return to filial piety and parental love.
If he abolishes artifice (ingenuity) and abandons (the pursuit of) profit there will be no more thieves and robbers.
Since, however, with these three alone one might think that adornments are too scanty, the people must be then given something additional:
Exhibit the plainness of undyed silk and embrace inwardly the simplicity of the uncarved block.
Reduce selfishness and lessen desires.

A sagacious and virtuous ruler does not seek cleverness and does not seek to rule by it. Since he already possesses the virtues of wisdom and sagacity, he is not seeking those qualities, not that those traits are negative by themselves. If a ruler possesses these qualities, the people will benefit from his rule much more than if he were to try to rule over them through cleverness and be only beginning to think of sagacity.

If a ruler is benevolent and of good deed by nature, rather than trying to acquire them [once he is in power], people will also naturally return to filial piety and parental love.

If those who are role models in society, especially those in power, avoid innovation combined with desire for profit and are loyal to tradition, the ugliness of theft will become evident, and society will no longer produce thieves.

However, it is possible that these three important principles, which are the virtues that must adorn a healthy life, may seem insignificant or even worthless. Thus, something additional must be added to these principles. Without mentioning explicitly what this is, Lao Tzu indicates by way of advice what must be added. Thus, he states that man must possess simplicity like plain and undyed silk, and embrace the spirit within him, which is simple like an uncarved block, and become united with it.

The chapter concludes with a verse that has a universal resonance. In an aphorism that is in fact the key to felicity, Lao Tzu says: reduce selfishness and lessen the desires of the carnal soul. They asked Bāyazīd Basṭāmi, "What do you want?" and he replied, "I want not to want."[40]

******

40. As quoted in, Rumi, *fihi mā fihi*, ed. Badīʿ al-zamān Foruzānfar, 5th ed. Tehran: 1386/1997, p. 104. For a description of Bāyazīd's life and spiritual station see, Farīd al-din ʿAṭṭār, *Tadhkirat al-awliyā*, ed. A. Tavakkolī, 4th ed. Tehran: 1375/1996, pp. 196-255.
ما تريدُ؟ أُريدُ أن لا أُريد

Chapter Twenty

Part I

Abandon learning (rules of good manner) and there will no longer be worries.
Between "yes" and "hum" how much difference is there?
Between good and evil, what distinction is there?

According to many commentators, "learning" in this context is an allusion to *li*, which denotes the proper social manners and etiquette that followers of the Confucian tradition value so highly. From the Taoist point of view, the more someone learns *li* and focuses on it, the more he will be anxious and upset over minor issues, and there is no limit to this feeling.

The allusion to the difference between the two words "yes" and "hum" is also related to formal social manners and etiquette, since they both mean the same thing. We can say that this statement and the one preceding it allude to the same truth that is emphasized so much in Sufism, namely, avoiding pretension, transcending outward forms, and concentrating on the inward.

Lao Tzu then turns to a fundamental mystical and ethical question. He asks, "What is the difference between good and evil?" which can also be translated "What is the difference between beauty and ugliness?" One cannot attain the Tao unless one can answer this fundamental question correctly.

Part II

"Whatever others respect, I must also respect."
Oh, how far away I am therefrom! For (on such a principle) there will be absolutely no limit to the vast field.
The multitude of people are happy and joyous as if taking part in a great feast, or as if enjoying the spring scenery from a high tower.
I alone remain still and silent, showing no sign of activity,
Like a newborn baby who has not yet learned to smile,
Forlorn and aimless, I am as if I had no place to return.
All others have more than enough.

I alone seem to be vacant and to have lost everything.
Mine is indeed the mind of a fool; how dull and confused it is.
The vulgar people are clever and bright; I alone am dull and dark.
The vulgar people are clever and sharp; I alone am dark and foggy.
Rising and falling like the deep sea I am.
Drifting like a wind that never stops at one place I am.
All others are busily engaged in doing something.
I alone am impractical and boorish.
I alone am different from others, for I value being fed by the Mother.

The first verse of this part is the quotation of a well-known statement in Chinese culture, not Lao Tzu's own teaching and must not be mistaken as such. It is mentioned here to make clear its falsehood, as is indicated by the second verse. "Being far" is not intended in a negative sense, but rather is meant to demonstrate how far from the truth the above statement is.

Ordinary people do not take life sufficiently seriously, and as the saying goes, they live in a fool's paradise, as if they are enjoying a grand party or appreciating a beautiful spring view from a high place. They are more concerned with fulfilling the desires of their carnal soul rather than elevating their spirit or acquiring true wisdom.

The subject of the verse beginning "I alone" is not any "I" but is the "I" of the sage, which alludes to his own I-ness (*anā'iyyah*), and as a sage he states that he is always calm and free of confusion, and does not identify himself with his outward actions. Thus, he states that he shows no sign of activity. In describing his inner state, he explains that he is like a newborn baby who is not yet able to smile. Even though he may experience happiness inwardly, his inner state is not revealed outwardly.

Like a wandering and aimless person, the sage may give the impression that he does not have a particular place that he belongs to and to which he can return. This statement can be interpreted as indicating that the sage is in the bosom of the Tao and needs no external place that belongs to him. In Sufism, the true home of the gnostic is the Divine Proximity, and thus nowhere else is his home, and yet he is at home wherever he is, for wherever he is "there is the luminous face of the Beloved."[41]

41. Ḥāfiẓ, op. cit., p. 44.

در عشقِ بین خانقاه و خرابات فرق نیست   هر جا که هست پرتو روی حبیب هست

In the abode of love no difference exists
between a tavern and a Sufi center
Wherever there is, there is
The luminous face of the Beloved.

In light of this truth, Lao Tzu adds that ordinary people have many, and in fact too many, attachments, while the sage is free from all attachments and empty of human concerns, "like someone who has lost everything."

> I am the slave of the will of the one who under the blue sky
> is free from anything that takes the color of attachment.[42]

The remaining verses of this chapter demonstrate the contrast and contradiction between the inner virtues, which are emphasized in Taoism, and the outward virtues of ordinary people, which are generally approved of and respected in society. In the context of this contrast, Lao Tzu calls himself foolish, intellectually dull, and confused, naming worldly people clever and bright, while he is dark and without light. Ordinary people, when it comes to worldly matters, are likewise clever and have bright ideas, while he, meaning the sage, lacks these qualities and has a foggy mind. Thus, he likens himself to a deep sea that is never calm and is constantly rising and falling. And likewise, he compares himself to a wind that is constantly drifting and never stops in one place.

By way of contrast, he mentions that others, that is, ordinary people, are all "busily engaged in doing something." It is only the sage who outwardly seems impractical and does not observe socially accepted manners, as is described in Islamic culture as the quality of being a *qalandar*.[43]

All these apparently negative descriptions are precisely only the outward appearance of things, since the last verse of this part begins by stating that the sage is "different from others," and ends with the foundational teaching that this difference is rooted in the fact that he only fundamentally values that which emanates upon him from the Tao. "Mother" in this verse is a symbol of the Way itself, the Tao.

******

42. Ḥāfiẓ, op. cit., p. 27.

43. A Qalandar is a free-spirited wandering dervish who is generally oblivious to the injunctions of the Shari'ah and often does not observe socially accepted rules of conduct and manners of social behavior. "The Qalandariyyah order was established by Jamal al-Din Sawaji (d. 1221) in the thirteenth century in Persia and Central Asia but spread to India and North Africa. Members of this order had a rough appearance with unruly, long hair and beard, and flouted habits of urban dwellers and prevalent social etiquette. They lived mostly in the countryside and some displayed psychic powers." S.H. Nasr, *The Garden of Truth*, New York: HarperColins, 2007, p. 194.

Chapter Twenty-One

In his behavior a man of all-pervading virtue follows the Tao
and the Tao alone.
The Tao in Its reality is a thing utterly obscure and utterly indistinct.
Utterly indistinct and utterly obscure; yet within It there is an Image.
Utterly obscure and utterly indistinct; yet within It there is Something.
Utterly profound and utterly dark; yet within It there is a Reality.
This Reality is extremely genuine. It contains within itself Its own proof.
From times of old till now Its Name has never left It.
Thereby, It governs the principles of all things.
How do I know that it is so with the principles of all things?
By means of this (that I have said).

In this chapter, Lao Tzu returns to the value of perfect virtue that a true sage possesses, adding this fundamental point that in his behavior not only does such a man follow the Tao, but also that he only follows the Tao. A man of God follows the teachings of the Divine Truth alone.

If the Tao is an obscure Reality, it is because it is not definable like other things. It is not a single reality among others such that it could be circumscribed, since it is infinite and cannot be encompassed. It is in this sense that Lao Tzu states that it is indistinct and is beyond any definable limit.

However, even though the Tao possesses these qualities, there is an image within it that is identifiable and definite. Again, Lao Tzu states that even though the Tao is utterly profound and utterly dark, meaning that It is beyond definition and comprehension, yet within It there is nevertheless a Reality, which, it must be added, can be known and accepted, since otherwise how could man know that It is Truth and not a falsehood parading as truth? In Islamic terminology, this is none other than the theophany (*tajallī*) of the Divine Essence (or the Principle of the Tao) that guides the sage towards to Tao Itself.

This Reality is indescribable, and Its nature is indescribably genuine. The ontological proof of this Reality is hidden within this

Reality Itself. The "Name" of this Reality, meaning Its quiddity and existence, has always been, and this Reality has never been without it. This quality has resulted in this Reality always governing all things. Then Lao Tzu asks, "How do I know" that the principles of all things govern all existents? The answer to this question is found in that which Lao Tzu has stated above.

******

Chapter Twenty-Two

"That which is crooked will remain unbent (perfect)."
That which is bent will become straight.
That which is hollow will become filled.
That which is worn out will become renewed.
If you have little, you will be given much.
If you have much, you will be worried.
Therefore, the sage embraces the One and becomes thereby
an exemplar for all things under Heaven.
He does not display himself; therefore, he shines out.
He does not consider himself right; therefore, he is illustrious.
He does not boast; therefore, he becomes the head.
It is because he does not contend with anyone that no one under
Heaven contends with him.
"That which is crooked will remain unbent (perfect)."
So did the ancients say.
How could this be an empty saying?
For in truth, it is by this principle that one can remain perfect till the end.

The first verse of this chapter refers to an ancient Chinese proverb, which explains that a crooked tree, since it is of no use to carpenters, will not be cut down and thus will remain intact. Lao Tzu then discusses the apparent movement towards perfection of various matters. Thus, he states that that which is bent will become straight, and that which is empty will be filled; and perhaps here the word "empty" is used in its ordinary sense, not in the Taoist meaning discussed previously. Similarly, a worn-out garment will be renewed, and that in it which is felt to be a defect will be compensated for and eventually removed. At the same time, Lao Tzu indicates that possessing more than one needs is not a blessing, and in fact causes anxiety of the mind and unease of the heart, as is commonly visible among the wealthy.

A sage is aware of all of these matters, and as a result of this awareness, as indicated by the word "therefore," distances himself from multiplicity and embraces the Unity of the Tao, that is, he becomes a true monotheist in the gnostic sense of this term. By doing so and reaching this spiritual station, he becomes the model or supreme exemplar for all existents. "Under Heaven" can be interpreted to mean creation, and "all things under Heaven" thus means the entirety of creation.

The word "self" in the phrase "he does not display himself" refers to the ego, the carnal soul (*nafs*), which is a veil over inwardness. If one does not expend one's effort displaying that veil, but rather avoids displaying it, the result is the removal of the veil over the inner light of the sage, and this unveiling will result in the radiance of this inner light becoming manifest.

He who has united with the One does not make pretentions to being right, not that he does not act rightly or is a criminal. Because he does not make pretentions to being right, he gains recognition and becomes illustrious, since such individuals are rare, and hence when they appear people recognize their value, and as a result they gain recognition without pretention or making efforts to become famous.

Boasting and self-aggrandizement are not the sign of perfection of the soul, but are rather signs of lack of virtue. Thus, even though those who praise themselves may possess certain virtues and positive qualities, these qualities will remain unknown. Conversely, the qualities of those who do not claim virtue and do not praise themselves will become evident, and the people will recognize and affirm them.

Individuals who possess perfection are never pretentious, and for this reason in whatever situation or position they may be they are always respected and "become the head" of affairs.

Ordinary life is always accompanied by competition, but the sage does not seek to compete with others. Rather, in all matters he seeks the truth and endeavors to act in accordance with it. As a result, others do not compete with him either. This statement does not negate the advice of various religions that invite people to compete doing good deeds and acquiring virtues rather than competing to acquire more material possessions than others.

After these ethical and philosophical teachings, Lao Tzu reiterates the Chinese proverb that he mentioned in the opening of this chapter, and in order to emphasize its truth asks, "How could this be an empty saying?" Finally, he adds that by recognizing the necessity of following the truth expressed, not only can one attain perfection (which is implied in this verse), but one can also remain in the station of perfection until the end of one's life.

******

Chapter Twenty-Three

Part I

Talking rarely, that is what is natural.
That is why a hurricane does not last a whole morning,
and a rainstorm does not last a whole day.
Who is it that causes all this?
Heaven and Earth.
If even Heaven and Earth cannot perpetuate (excessive states),
much less can man.

The nature of a virtuous man or one who lives in accordance with his primordial nature is to rarely speak and not be loquacious.

Speak rarely and speak choice words, like pearls
So that from thy speech the world will be filled.[44]

Speaking rarely, however, is not absolute silence, and thus the sage speaks when necessary but without allowing this state to become constant and turn into loquaciousness. To illustrate this, Lao Tzu presents the example of a hurricane that arrives with force and noise but does not last long, and of a rainstorm that does not last the entire day. This is of course in reference to the climate of China, or of a region like Iran, not to tropical or sub-tropical regions where, as is the case of the monsoon in India, rain can continue for days on end.

Lao Tzu then poses the question, what is the reason that a hurricane is short-lived? He answers that this is the structure of the cosmos, as is indicated by his mention of Heaven and Earth. He draws the ethical conclusion from this: if Heaven and Earth set a limit for the roaring of a hurricane, man must all the more set a limit to his own voice.

44. Niẓāmī Ganjawī, *Laylī-u Majnūn*, ed. Waḥīd Dastgirdī, Tehran, Armaghān, 1313/1934, p. 45.

کم گوی و گزیده گوی چون درّ   تا زاندك تو جهان شود پر

Part II

In the cause of pursuing the Tao, he who has attained the stage of the Tao becomes identical with the Tao, and he who has attained the stage of the Virtue becomes identical with the Virtue; whereas he who has lost the Tao and the Virtue becomes identical with the lost.
He who is identical with the Tao is gladly accepted by the Tao;
He who is identical with the Virtue is gladly accepted by the Virtue;
He who is identical with something lost is gladly accepted by the thing lost.

Attaining the Tao involves a process, which is none other than spiritual wayfaring. When this wayfaring reaches its destination, union with the Divine Truth takes place, and the sage "becomes identical with the Tao," meaning that he is not separate from it. As such he can say, "Who am I? Laylī. And who is Laylī? She is I,"[45] and, "There is nothing in my robe other than God."[46]

Likewise, he who attains virtue becomes identical with it. But conversely, he who loses virtue and the Tao, naturally becomes identical with the state of loss, and no longer considers himself identical with the Tao and virtue. If one attains the station of union with the Tao, he will be embraced by it with open arms. From a spiritual point of view, it can also be said that if one is not accepted by God, he cannot attain the station of union with Him. Likewise, he who attains union with virtue will be embraced by virtue with open arms. However, he who distances himself from the Tao and virtue considers himself one with the state of loss and is embraced by this state of forgetfulness with open arms.

Part III

If one is not trusted enough, that is because one is not truthful enough.

Lao Tzu concludes this chapter by stating that trustworthiness is a necessary quality. As such, he considers the cause of one losing the trust of others, which is none other than a lack of truthfulness and honesty. If one is not honest, naturally others will not trust him. There is a close connection between trust and honesty, and this is inevitable and is visible in all human societies.

45. Rūmī, *Mathnawī*, V:2018.
من کیم لیلی و لیلی کیست من   ما یکي روحیم انبر دو بدن
46. Famously attributed to both al-Ḥallāj and Bayazīd Bastāmī.
ليس في جبتي سوي الله

Chapter Twenty-Four

Part I

He who stands on tiptoe cannot stand firm.
He who strides cannot walk far.
He who displays himself cannot shine forth.
He who considers himself right cannot be prominent.
He who praises himself can have no merit.
He who boasts cannot endure.

This chapter discusses that which is contrary to walking the straight path. As such, Lao Tzu states that the result of standing on tiptoe is instability and in this condition one cannot stand firmly. Thus, one must depend on one's whole foot in order to stand firmly and continuously. Similarly, one who walks with speed cannot continue in this way for long or traverse a great distance. Thus, one must stand firmly, walk at a moderate pace, and avoid hastening.

In his discussion on avoiding excess, Lao Tzu returns to a topic that he had alluded to previously, namely showing off. He mentions indirectly that the human soul is not like a lamp that will more completely illuminate its surroundings if it shines more brightly; rather the opposite is the case. The more one shows off, the less it shines. Pretentiousness and pride do not make one shine forth and become distinguished. Likewise, those who always consider themselves to be right and are not objective in judging themselves and others cannot gain prominence among people. This is a remarkable ethical principle: showing off diminishes man's eminence, whereas in the world of nature anything that is more apparent becomes more prominent.

The verse that follows is an expression of the same truth in a different language. Thus, Lao Tzu explains that self-praise and pretension indeed diminish man's prominence rather than enhancing it. Pretension is closely related to self-praise, which not only does not make one distinguished, but also cannot be permanent, for by nature it is transient.

Part II

From the point of view of the Tao all these attitudes are so-called
"leftover goods and useless tumors."
They are detested by most living beings.
Therefore, he who possesses the Tao does not ever take such an attitude.

After mentioning all of these negative qualities with contemptible language, Lao Tzu likens all of these inclinations to leftover food and useless tumors[47] that one leaves on one's plate and avoids eating. Moreover, not only is this detested by the one who eats the meal, but also by other creatures which are reluctant to eat it. He concludes that he who attains union with the Divine Truth and "possesses the Tao" never eats this rejected food or puts himself in a position where he would have to eat it. This verse of course has a spiritual meaning that goes beyond material food. The seeker of wisdom seeks to absorb real food of the spirit, rather than leftovers that lack the power to nourish his spirit.

******

47. "useless tumors": this is a term in Taoism and refers to certain attitudes as useless or meaningless. The description is in the text

Chapter Twenty-Five

Part I

There is something formless and perfect,
born before Heaven and Earth.
Silent and void, It stands alone never changing,
It goes around everywhere, never becoming exhausted.
It is to be considered the "Mother" of Heaven and Earth.
I know not Its Name.
Forging a pseudonym I call it the Tao.
Being forced to name It, I would call It "Great."
"Great" would imply Its "moving forward."
"Moving forward" would imply Its "extending farther and farther away."
"Extending farther and farther away" would imply coming back
to Its original point.

The Reality that was before Heaven and Earth and that is formless while being perfect is the Tao on the level of Its creativity with regard to the realm of existence. It is similar to what in Sufism is called the Breath of the Compassionate (*nafas al-Raḥmān*). If the verb "birth" is mentioned with regard to It, it is not in the ordinary meaning of the term; rather, what is intended is "possessing being"; not that there was a time when It did not exist, since that Reality is the Tao Itself with regard to its creative power of existentiating Heaven and Earth. It is for this reason that in this verse it is said that this Reality Itself is beyond sound, meaning external determinations, and thus It is empty in the Taoist sense of the term and without change or transformation. Its manifestations undergo change and transformation, but It Itself is still and unchanging.

It is present everywhere, which is what is meant by "It goes around everywhere." It does not diminish, as is indicated by the words "never becoming exhausted." It is known as the "Mother" of Heaven and Earth, that is, Heaven and Earth are born from that Reality.

The first part of this chapter refers to the principle discussed in the first chapter of the *Tao Te Ching*, which states, "The Name that can be named is not the eternal Name." The last verse of this part affirms this truth: that the Divine Essence has no name and no description. Therefore, Its name cannot be known, which is to say one cannot affirm of It any determination. This verse refers to the Reality and Essence of the Tao at Its highest level, and not on the level of the existentiating principle of Heaven and Earth.

Part II

Hence the Tao is great, Heaven is great, Earth is great, and the king is also great.
Within the boundaries of the world of being there are four things that are great, and the king counts as one of them.

If Lao Tzu says that the name "Tao" is only metaphorical, it is to emphasize that the Reality of the Tao is beyond name. Otherwise, from an authentic religious perspective, in various religions the Name of God is revealed by God Himself and has an inner unity with the Named, and hence man takes recourse to this Name in worship. This truth must not be mistaken with the fact that the Divine Essence is beyond name. Thus, man takes recourse to the Attribute of Greatness, as when in Islam we say, "God is the Greatest" (*Allāhu akbar*) and speak of the Divine Grandeur (*kibriyā*).

The Tao's "moving forward" does not suggest advancement or progress in the modern sense, which was invented by the modernist worldview. Here what is meant is that the Tao embraces all things, and especially that of the passage of time, through which each day a new page in the book of creation is turned. The Tao remains present in the manifestation of new phenomena, such that there is not a single page in the book of existence in which the Tao is not present.

In this verse, there is an allusion to the preceding verse that considers the continuing necessity and passage of time, which moves farther and farther away; yet the presence of the Tao within it remains. Furthermore, since the journey of existence is cyclical and existents return to their Origin and Source, Lao Tzu emphasizes this "extending farther and farther away," which in the end results in coming back to the original point.

Part III

Man models himself on Earth.
Earth models itself on Heaven.
Heaven models itself on the Tao.
And the Tao models Itself on its own intrinsic nature.

This part of the *Tao Te Ching* is very well-known, and here Lao Tzu clearly expresses the levels of existence (*silsilah-yi marātib-i wūjūd*) in accordance with the perennial philosophy (*ḥikmat-i khālidah*), though naturally in the language of Chinese philosophy. He begins with man, stating that Earth, in the Chinese cosmological sense, is man's archetype. That is to say, man is the manifestation of realities on Earth, again in the traditional Chinese meaning that Lao Tzu has previously explained. In the same way, the Earth is the manifestation of the realities of Heaven, and Heaven, again in the cosmological sense, is the manifestation of the realities of the Tao. Ultimately, it is only the Tao of which the reality is Its very Self. The reality of the Tao is only Tao Itself. There is a clear similarity here between these levels and the "Five Divine Presences" (*ḥaḍarāt-i khamsah-yi ilāhīyyah*) of Sufism.[48]

******

48. "The Five Divine Presences, which are another way to indicate the hierarchy of being, are enumerated and described by Ibn 'Arabī as follows: one, *Hāhūt*, the "level" of the Supreme Essence of the Divinity; two, *Lāhūt*, the level of Divine Names and Attributes and Being as the ontological principle of creation; three, *Jabarūt*, the archangelic level and the higher paradisal worlds as well as the created logos; four, *malakūt*, the subtle domain and the imaginal world standing immediately above this world but stretching to the paradisal realm; and five, *nāsū* or *mulk*, which corresponds to the human, material, and terrestrial world." See Seyyed Hossein Nasr, *The Garden of Truth: The Vision and Promise of Sufism, Islam's Mystical Tradition*, HarperCollins, 2007, pp. 49-50.

Chapter Twenty-Six

What is heavy is the root of what is light.
What is calm is the master of what is restless.
Therefore, the sage, though travelling all day (on a carriage), never leaves the (heavily laden) baggage carts out of sight.
Even in the midst of magnificent sights, he remains peaceful, tranquil and detached.
How then should a ruler of ten thousand chariots treat his own person more lightly than the empire (under his rule)?
If he behaves lightly, he loses his subjects.
If he is restless, he loses his lordship.

Here, heaviness should not be understood to allude to material affairs, nor lightness to the spirit and psyche. Rather, heaviness refers to the quality of the Origin and Principle, and lightness to its manifestations. In the terminology of Islamic philosophy, this verse can be interpreted to mean that Absolute Being is the origin and source of all existent things in the world of becoming (*'alam-i ṣayrūrat*) and all the levels below Pure Being. Since Absolute Being is beyond movement and becoming, it has mastery over the restless world that is in the constant state of motion of becoming.

The heavy load mentioned in this verse is a metaphor for the same heavy Reality that is alluded to in the first verse of the chapter. Hence, Lao Tzu states that the sage, whose gaze is always directed towards Absolute Being, while travelling, indicating life and which is accompanied by becoming on the human plane, is never negligent of that heavy load, that is, the Origin of Being. Through the journey of this world he is changing, yet his gaze is towards the world of permanence, and on the highest level, on Being Itself. Thus, even while experiencing magnificent sights or the glamour of the world, the sage never loses his inner tranquility, which is the result of his attachment to the higher degrees of existence and Absolute Being Itself, and has no sense of attachment to transient matters. That is to say, he is "free from anything that takes the color of attachment."[49]

It is in light of this important principle of attachment to the immutable and eternal Truth and not to transient realities that Lao Tzu returns to social and political realities, asking how it is possible that a king, with all the arms of war that he possesses, would treat himself with less attention, more superficially and more lightly than the kingdom over which he rules. From a spiritual point of view, one must first rule over oneself according to correct principles in order to be able to rule over others. In response to this question, he states that the result of the ruler treating himself lightly is losing the subjects over whom he rules, and if he cannot rule through his access to a being that is beyond the commotion of the world of becoming, but rather lives and acts restlessly, he will fall from his position of authority.

******

49. Ḥāfiẓ, *Dīwān*, ibid.

Chapter Twenty-Seven

One who walks well leaves no tracks.
One who speaks well makes no flaws.
One who counts well uses no counter rods.
One who closes well uses no bolts and bars,
Yet, what he has closed cannot be opened.
One who ties well uses no cords and knots.
Yet, what he has tied cannot be undone.
Likewise, the sage is always good at saving people.
He leaves no one abandoned and unsaved.
He is always good at saving things.
He leaves nothing abandoned and unused.
This is what I would call doubling one's natural light.
Thus the good man is the teacher of the bad man and the bad man is for the good man a useful means.
He who does not value his own teacher, or he who does not love his own means, no matter how clever he might be, is in fact grossly mistaken.
This is what I would consider the most essential and subtle truth.

The first few verses of this chapter are Taoist commentaries on ordinary actions. Thus, Lao Tzu begins by speaking of walking. The footsteps of one who walks well from a spiritual point of view will not be heavy, but will be calm and light, and as a result leave no tracks. This statement is reminiscent of Christ's saying, "Walk gently on the earth." The human spirit lacks heaviness, while the body is heavy. From a gnostic point of view, walking lightly alludes to the dominance of man's spirit over his body.

Similarly, Lao Tzu states that he who has the ability to speak well can express what he wishes without error. At first glance, this verse concerns the outward aspect of speaking, but it also has an inner meaning: speaking well is inseparable from truth and free from falsehood.

Again in connection with the same topic, he indicates that he who has mastery over accounting has no need of outward instruments of calculation, such as a counting rod or an abacus, which were common in ancient times in China as in Iran. That is, within himself and without making use of external instruments, he takes account of everything correctly.

Finally, alluding to the same truth and in light of the connection between cause and effect, Lao Tzu adds that a door shut properly does not need a lock. Whilst referring to doors in the external world, this also indicates the inner door of man's spirit, soul, and thought. Then he affirms that a door that is closed well, whether it be an outer or inner door, is guaranteed the protection of not being opened.

The art of skillful packing does not require cords and knots. This art is still alive in the Far East, and can be seen in the art of packaging goods such that even without thread or rope there is no danger of them opening accidentally when transported. The verse at the same time has a symbolic meaning connected to the deep perception of the truth, after which there is no danger of it "opening" or being lost.

All these qualities are reflected in the characteristics of the sage, who is skilled in saving people. He has this skill because he possesses all the virtues mentioned in previous verses of this chapter. The sage is always active in endeavoring to save others, never abandoning people in their flawed condition or in ignorance and falsehood. Since he possesses wisdom, he is granted Divine Success (*tawfiq*) in preserving that which is positive. Lao Tzu then reiterates that the sage never ignores that which is needed, leaving it unused and unfruitful. He describes the sage's way of acting as a means to strengthen and double the natural light that exists within his being.

Furthermore, the sage, or the man of good nature, is a teacher, not only for good people, but also for bad people, while bad people are a means for the sage to teach goodness and to transform evil into good. The important point is for one to appreciate the value of a good teacher and to have the desire to overcome one's difficulties and transcend one's inner limitations. Otherwise, mere cleverness is not sufficient for one to solve one's own problems, and by relying on one's cleverness alone one will go astray and make grave errors.

The author of the *Tao Te Ching* considers that which is discussed in this chapter to be the most essential and subtle truth, and by stating this, affirms the importance of this chapter for acquiring wisdom and gnosis.

******

Chapter Twenty-Eight

He who knows the male, yet keeps to the role of the female,
will become the ravine of the whole world.
Once he has become the ravine of the whole world, then the eternal Virtue (of the Tao) will not desert him and he will again return to the state of infancy.
He who knows the white, yet keeps to the role of the black,
will become the model for all under Heaven.
Once he has become the model for the whole world,
then the state of Virtue will never betray him.
And he will again return to the Limitless.
He who knows the glorious, yet keeps to the role of the disgraced,
will become the valley of all under Heaven.
Once he has become the valley of the whole world,
then he will be replete with the eternal Virtue.
And he will again return to the state of the uncarved block.
The uncarved block, when it is hollowed out, becomes various vessels.
Likewise, the sage, by making use of it, becomes the lord
of all officials and chiefs.
Hence the greatest product is that which is still uncut.

The feminine and masculine principles (Yin & Yang) are fundamental components of the Chinese worldview, and in many respects are comparable to the doctrine of the Divine Names of Majesty and Beauty in Sufism. All human beings, male or female, participate in both Yin and Yang. If man is aware of Yang and at the same time remains faithful to the feminine principle within, he will become a ravine for the entire world. A ravine or valley is a location for human life and all its activities, and a sage who is aware of both the masculine principle and the feminine principle and remains faithful to it is like that ravine containing all activities of life.

He who becomes like a ravine will always possess eternal virtue, which in fact is precisely the Tao. He will return to a childlike state, which indicates innocence of spirit and soul. It is in this sense that Christ said that one must be childlike to enter Heaven, meaning free of all sins and with an innocent spirit.[50] It is worthy of note that one of most important treatises of Shihāb al-Dīn Suhrawardī is entitled *On the States of Childhood* (*Fī aḥwāl al-ṭufūliyyah*).

Blackness can allude both to that which is below existence, of which the symbol is the color white, and also that which is beyond Being and its manifestations, and which is termed non-existence in Taoist language. This was alluded to at the beginning of the *Tao Te Ching* in the description of the one who knows the world of existence and yet is immersed in the non-existence beyond-Being. This non-existence, which in Sufism is termed "black light," is the archetype of perfection for all that is in the realm of existence and "under Heaven."

He who reaches such a spiritual station and becomes a model for the whole world possesses eternal virtue, and this virtue will never desert him. Such a person returns to the Origin of existence, which has no limit; It is Infinite and Absolute.

Wisdom and good nature are accompanied by glory. If one reaches such a station but presents himself as one of the people of blame (*ahl-i malāmat*), not claiming glory or showing off, he has attained perfection and thus a valley for all existents, like the ravine described above. This statement of Lao Tzu about the people of blame is remarkably similar to the teachings of Ibn 'Arabī and certain other masters of Sufism. Ibn 'Arabī states that among those in whose being the Truth has been realized, the *malāmiyyah* or the *malāmatiyyah*, meaning the people of blame, possess the highest spiritual station. The role of the people of blame in Islamic history is considerably similar to an important level of Chinese spirituality. The being of one who reaches such a spiritual station and becomes a valley for others is filled with eternal virtue.

Here Lao Tzu refers again to the uncarved block of wood, a block of wood that has not yet become determined [in a particular form], meaning existence beyond its determinations. This verse reminds the reader that this block of wood has not yet been carved, and when it is carved it will take on various forms, meaning that whenever Pure Being is determined it emerges as this or that existing thing. The sage is that very uncarved block of wood who, using the reality of the wood, acquires power in the terrestrial world (*'ālam-i nāsūt*), possessing dominance over those who rule and lead the people. This verse in fact expresses the ideal of the Taoist tra-

50. Matthew, 18:3.

dition, which is that the sage should govern over those who have authority in human societies. The conclusion of this exposition is that the most precious thing, or in Lao Tzu's terms "product," is the wood that has not yet been carved and taken on a particular form. This is precisely Being, which possesses the highest value beyond its existential manifestations.

******

Chapter Twenty-Nine

Part I

When a man intends to take the whole world, having recourse to
various artifices, I know from the beginning
that he cannot accomplish this task.
The world is a sacred vessel and nobody can shape it by artifice.
Whosoever tries to shape it will only damage it.
Whosoever remains attached to it will finally lose it.

All the verses of this part are reminders of the principle of non-action and detachment to which Lao Tzu has alluded previously and, in sum, present the Taoist belief in the sanctity of nature and the need to respect it rather than dominate it. The endeavor to dominate nature using man-made technologies and artifices is impossible and will eventually result in catastrophe. Ultimately, this endeavor is futile, as it is beyond human capabilities. It is as if Lao Tzu composed these verses for modern man, whose main objective is to subjugate nature for his own benefit.

Lao Tzu reminds us that the cosmos is a sacred reality, and that man does not have the power to do with it whatever he desires and rebuild it according to his own wishes. It should also be added that, from the traditional point of view, the final word belongs to nature and not to man. Modern man does not accept this view, and of course there were certain individuals in ancient times who thought likewise, but it was not as in the present age such that they were in the majority.

Bearing in mind this truth, Lao Tzu reminds us that the attempt to shape this "sacred vessel" will result in damaging it, as we are now witnessing with the emergence of the environmental crisis. The sacred vessel is none other than nature created by God according to the perspective of the Abrahamic religions.

Therefore, one must indeed be the "the slave of the will of the one who...is free from anything that takes the color of attachment."[51] He who wishes to make the world depend on him

51. Ḥāfiẓ, *Dīwān*, ibid.

will ultimately lose it altogether. In the language of Islamic philosophy, the world belongs to God alone, and not to man, who is only a guest, inhabiting it for a few short days.

Part II

He who intends to go in front ends by falling behind.
He who blows on something to make it warm ends by making it cold.
He who intends to become strong ends by becoming weak.
He who intends to destroy (others) ends by being destroyed.
In view of this fact, the sage avoids excess, extravagance.

The subject of this part is a repetition of the Taoist principle that a refined man must be like water, which seeks the lowest ground and flows there instead of endeavoring to get in front and take the lead. Thus, Lao Tzu states that whoever makes an effort to go in front against the downward flow of water, will end by falling behind. If such a person tries to heat something, the opposite will result, and that thing will become cool. If he works hard to gain power, which is to say outward, material power and not spiritual power, he will be faced with his own weakness. And if he seeks to defeat and destroy someone, in the end he will destroy himself. In all these cases, the result is the opposite of what outward intelligence and cleverness would predict.

Lao Tzu finally concludes that a sage who is aware of this truth travels the opposite path to that taken by ordinary people, eschewing excess in worldly affairs and luxuries, and detesting vainglory and extravagance, which is the mother of many a corruption of the soul. Mentioning this quality at the end of the list of negative character traits is also an affirmation of the potential of this vicious quality to dominate over the mind and soul of man.

******

Chapter Thirty

Part I

One who assists the ruler through the Tao does not strengthen the state by force of arms. For this kind of thing is liable to rebound.
Wherever armies have encamped, there brambles and thorns grow.
In the wake of a great war, there always comes a lean year of famine.

The possessor of wisdom who wishes to help the governing power and the ruler through the Tao cannot do so by strengthening the armed forces. If he does so, the result will most likely be negative and there will be no actual help. The philosophical proof for this is that wherever someone resorts to force and deploys the armed forces, problems result, and "there brambles and thorns grow." Along the same lines, Lao Tzu adds that a great war is always followed by periods of tribulation, of which famine is a sign. Aggression and hostility always have negative consequences. "O slain one, whom did you slay such that they slayed you?"[52]

Part II

So a good (general) brings (his campaign) to completion
and stops there.
He does not proceed further with warfare.
Having completed his work, he does not become boastful.
Having concluded his work, he does not become conceited.
Having concluded his work, he does not become arrogant.
Having concluded his work, he does not become ruthless.
Remember whatever has reached the height of vigor necessarily
falls into decrepitude.
This manner of doing things is to go against the Tao
Whatever goes against the Tao will soon come to an end.

52. Nāṣir Khusraw, *Dīwān-i Ash'ār-i Dīwān-i Ḥakīm Nāṣir Khusraw Qubādiyānī*, ed. Mujtabā Mīnuwī and Mahdī Muḥaqqiq, p. 519. "Whom did you kill, to be killed yourself in a miserable way, or who will kill the one who killed you?"

عیسی به رهی دید یکی کشته فتاده   حیران شد و بگرفت به دندان سر انگشت
گفتا که کرا کشتی تا کشته شدي زار   تا باز که اورا بکشد آنکه تورا کشت؟

A true warrior does not go to war for the sake of war. In the same way, a virtuous general ceases his activity immediately once he has attained his objective in a battle and does not seek further campaigns. Thus, after attaining this goal he does not continue the war.

The next four verses are devoted to a description of the mental and spiritual state of such a general after the war has been concluded. He does not praise himself or boast, does not lose his humility or become proud, and does not lose his capacity for compassion. It is as if these verses of the *Tao Te Ching* describe 'Alī ibn Abī Ṭālib, who was an unmatched warrior and peerless general.

After mentioning these qualities of a virtuous general, Lao Tzu reminds us of this universal principle, that anything that "reach[es] the height of vigor necessarily falls into decrepitude," much like a fountain, which, according to the Persian proverb, flows down once it reaches its peak.[53] Struggling to reach the peak, not only in war but in life in general, is against the reality of the Tao. Whatever is against the reality of the Tao has no permanence and will cease to exist after a short while.

******

---

53. A famous Persian proverb.
فواره چون بلند شود سرنگون شود

Chapter Thirty-One

Part I

Good arms are instruments of ill omen. Everyone detests them.
Therefore, the man possessed of Tao is not at ease with using them.

In war, naturally the best armaments possible are used, yet such instruments of war are inauspicious, and the people detest them even as they try to use them. They detest them because they know that this type of weaponry will cause more death, even of their own soldiers, since the enemy may also use these effective weapons and casualties will not be limited to the opposing and defeated forces alone. This is all the more true in the modern period with all of its new weapons of mass destruction. If it were not for the terrible weapons of the modern era, ninety million people would not have been killed in the Second World War. Therefore, whoever is possessed of the Tao in his own being is reluctant to use good arms, and even if he is forced to do so, he is not at ease with using them.

Part II

The noble man when at home considers the left as the higher position,
But in time of war the right is considered as the higher position.
Arms are instruments of ill omen.
They are not the instruments of a nobleman.
When one is forced to use them, it is best to do so without attaching importance to them.

Since in Chinese philosophy Yin is associated with the left, whoever possesses nobility will consider the left as superior while in his own house. However, in times of war, the natural order is reversed, and as a result Yang, which is associated with the right hand, takes the higher position.

In the Taoist world view, which is based on peace and serenity, weapons are considered instruments of corruption and ill omens, and hence have a negative connotation. As a result, such weapons are not the instruments of a noble man. However, the question arises, what is the noble man to do when conditions arise that render using instruments of war necessary?

The answer to this question, which is implied in this verse, is found in the verse that follows it: if conditions arise in which one is forced to use such armaments, he has no choice but to use them, but while doing so he does not give them any importance. That is, he does not allow his existence to be dependent upon them and he distances himself from them inwardly.

Part III

Victory is not something to be glorified.
To glorify it despite this is to take delight in the slaughtering of men.
But one who takes delight in the slaughtering of men will never accomplish his intention in the world.

On attaining victory, one should not become joyous and consider one's success as something to be glorified. If one does so, the pleasure of victory will become established in one's mind, and the pleasure of killing will take root in one's being, prompting one to continue killing. He who takes pleasure in killing and is constantly engaged in war will never be able to achieve his intention in life because the thirst for blood will remain within him and will not be quenched by further killing.

Part IV

On auspicious occasions, the left is considered the higher position, whereas on inauspicious occasions the right is considered the higher position.
This is why the lieutenant is posted on the left and the general is posted on the right. This means that in pursuing warfare one is observing funeral rites.
If a great number of people are killed in war, one would weep over it, filled with sorrow.
When one gains victory in war, one should observe the rites of mourning.

In this verse, Lao Tzu returns to the symbolism of right and left in Chinese philosophy, stating that the symbolic meaning of the left is auspiciousness and that of the right is inauspiciousness. Thus, it is natural for people to consider the left hand superior in times of peace and security, and to view the right as superior in inauspicious times of hardship and misery. This categorization of left and right is contrary to what is found in Indo-European and Semitic languages and cultures, in which words such as "right," *rāst* and *yamīn* have a positive connotation, whereas "left" suggests the opposite, as one sees in the terms "the companions of the right" and "the companions of the left" in the Quran. This symbolism of the right and left must not be mistaken with Lao Tzu's explanation.

In light of this teaching of Chinese philosophy, Lao Tzu states that at the time of war the lieutenant is posted on the left and the general is posted on the right, since in war the natural relationship between left and right is reversed. However, this verse does not mean that a lieutenant is superior to a general in terms of rank.

The reversal of natural relationships in times of war demands that people not celebrate after a victory, but rather sit in mourning until the situation returns to normal. Even if victory is achieved in war, many will have been killed and the people will weep over this, filled with sorrow, despite the victory.

This chapter concludes by once again reminding us that participation in mourning rites for those who have died in war is necessary despite victory. This reality is so fundamental that even in modern times, despite traditional teachings having been forgotten, even those who have been victorious mourn for those who have been lost.

******

Chapter Thirty-Two

Part I

Tao in its eternity is nameless.
The uncarved block may appear insignificant, but no one in the world is able to subjugate it.
Should kings and lords manage to hold fast to it, the Ten Thousand Things will of themselves come to pay homage to them.
Heaven and Earth will join their forces and send down sweet dew.
The people of themselves will become peacefully governed even though no decrees and ordinances are published.

As mentioned previously, like many other revealed books, the *Tao Te Ching* repeats certain fundamental truths in different chapters, as is the case here. Lao Tzu states that in Its eternity the Tao is nameless, meaning that It has no delimitation. Also as in other chapters, here Lao Tzu returns to the symbol of the uncarved block of wood, meaning substance that has not yet been delimited. Since It has not taken a particular form, It seems insignificant, yet It can never be subjugated, for It is the foundation of all things.

True power originates from Tao. Thus, if those who possess authority in society hold fast to the Tao and are not separated from It, all beings will submit to them, and, to use the language of the text, will "pay homage to them," which is to say that they will be respected by all. The status of such individuals is so exalted that all beings from Heaven to Earth will unite to bestow upon them sweet drops of dew (indicating divine emanation and blessing). If such individuals govern society, society will be managed properly even without the rulers issuing any commands, since the authority of governance is based on the governance of the Tao, which is the principle of all people and all things.

Part II

Only when it (the uncarved block) is cut out, then there are names.
As soon as the names have come into being, we must know where to stop.
Knowing where to stop means being free from danger.

The relation of the Tao to the things under Heaven may be compared to the rivulets and streams all flowing into the River and the Ocean.

This part illuminates the difference between the root and its branches, between the Truth and Its applications. As such, Lao Tzu states that it is only once an uncarved block of wood is carved, or once existence is determined through the receptacles of different forms, that names, meaning forms in the philosophical sense, are manifested. When one enters the realm of forms and determinations, the need to determine limits in various domains arises and the fundamental question presents itself of where to stop. If one does not pay proper attention to this question, he will drown in the shoreless ocean of becoming, and multiplicity will prevent him from perceiving unity.

One of the most important teachings of traditional wisdom is precisely this knowledge of how much one must devote oneself to multiplicities and where to stop. Knowing this saves us from the danger of drowning in the world of relativity and forgetfulness of the Absolute.

All rivers eventually return to the ocean, and awareness of the Tao in relation to all beings brings about the awareness of this fundamental truth that "all things return to their Origin" (*kullu shay'in yarji'u ilā aṣlihi*), which is the Tao Itself.

******

Chapter Thirty-Three

He who knows others is clever, but he who knows himself is enlightened.
He who conquers others is forceful, but he who conquers himself is really powerful.
He who knows contentment is rich.
He who perseveres is a man of will.
He who does not lose his proper place will endure long.
He who dies but does not perish is the one who has real longevity.

Through cleverness one can gain a superficial knowledge of something other than oneself, but for deep knowledge it is necessary to have self-knowledge, which makes one enlightened. In traditional wisdom, truly knowing the other is dependent upon knowing oneself, in contrast to that which is seen in modern science, in which effort is made to know the other without importance being given to knowing oneself.

> Do not seek to be clever, attain perplexity.
> Cleverness is conjecture, perplexity a triumph.[54]

If one conquers another, naturally he has the power to do so and thus is strong. However, more difficult than conquering others is conquering one's own self. Thus, Lao Tzu states that he who achieves victory over his own soul is truly powerful and possesses more power to attain victory over others.

He who attains the blessing of being content with what he has is truly rich, since he needs nothing else. The Quran states "God is the rich and you are the poor." To understand this truth is to achieve the spiritual station of poverty in the spiritual sense, and this truth itself makes one rich, for by attaining this station one becomes independent of all other than God. The mention of being rich in the Chinese text alludes to this same reality, namely a richness that is precisely in the awareness of the inherent poverty of man and the richness of the Tao.

---

54. Rūmī, *Mathnawī*, IV:1407.
زيركي ظن است و حيرانى ظفر　　　زيركي كم جوي و حيرانى بخر

Enduring hardships and persevering is not possible without having a strong will and using this will in confronting challenges. Using one's will also depends on the virtues of endurance of hardship and perseverance in attaining one's goal.

The one who possesses a station that is appropriate for his abilities, and not above it, is felicitous. Such an individual is not quickly removed from his position, but rather maintains it for a long time. This verse indicates the famous Chinese belief that in the perfect society each person holds a position appropriate to his condition.

The last verse of this chapter appears enigmatic, but in Chinese philosophy true longevity does not only mean having a long life in this world, but also alludes to eternal life after the death of the body. This verse is in fact a definition of "true longevity," and not perishing is not simply an allusion to the enduring of one's name after death but to the enduring of the spirit.

******

Chapter Thirty-Four

The great Tao is like a thing drifting on the water.
It goes everywhere left and right.
The Ten Thousand Things depend upon It for coming into being; yet It does not boast of It.
It accomplishes Its task; yet makes no claim.
It clothes and feeds the Ten Thousand Things; yet never domineers over them.
Being eternally free of desire, It may be called Small.
The Ten Thousand Things go back to It; yet It makes no claim to dominate over them. In this respect It may be called Great.
But It never considers Itself great. Therefore, Its greatness is perfect.

Something that drifts on water goes this way and that. It is everywhere and yet is not in any specific place. Thus, Lao Tzu likens the great Tao to a thing that drifts on moving water. It is everywhere, yet is not in any specific place.

In light of this, Lao Tzu adds that the Tao is moving in all directions, from right to left and left to right. He then repeats a principle to which he has alluded before, that the ten thousand existents, meaning the world of existence below the Origin, "depend on It" to acquire being and set foot in the domain of existence. That is to say, without the Tao they will not be manifested. However, the Tao does not boast about this fundamental truth, and "naturally" gives them existence.

The Tao *as such* accomplishes the task of bestowing existence and being a guide for the realm of existence without making any claim, since such action is rooted in the nature and substance of the Tao.

The Tao clothes and "gives daily bread" to all beings, which is to say that It makes their existence and their essential activities possible, not by domineering over them in the usual sense of the word, but by giving existence to them. Or: bestowing existence upon them.

One must not attribute desire in the human sense of the term to the Tao. As such, Lao Tzu calls the Tao "Small," though this of course is not in relation to the reality of the Tao. The Ten Thousand Things, which is to say, all existents, will ultimately return to their Origin, which is precisely the Tao. However, the Tao never claims to dominate over them; rather, this return is itself part of the order of creation. Since all things return to the Tao, one can call It not only "Small" but also "Great," and in Islamic terms say *Allāhu Akbar* (God is the Greatest).

The last verse presents a moral lesson that since the Tao does not consider Itself to be great, Its greatness is perfect. The verse must not be mistaken with the metaphysical truth that the Origin is essentially great, or is greater than any concept that man can have of greatness. As such, we must differentiate between this gnostic and religious truth and the practical lesson that Lao Tzu presents in the verse.

******

Chapter Thirty-Five

He who goes through the world holding in hand the Great Image,
Wherever he may go, he will meet with no harm.
Safe, tranquil and calm he will remain.
Beautiful music and delicious food induce the wayfarers to stop.
But the Tao, uttered in words, is insipid and without any flavor.
One looks at It, and finds It unworthy to be seen.
One listens to It, and finds It unworthy to be heard.
Yet, when one uses It, one finds It inexhaustible.

The "Great Image" is a formless form. Delimited without being delimited, It is the ladder of ascent from multiplicity to unity. Thus, possessing It places one on a plane of existence that is other than the ordinary plane of existence. If one takes recourse to It, in according with the Quranic command "hold fast to the rope of God,"[55] he will be immune from every harm and affliction. As the Persian proverb states, "Be with God and do whatever you want."

No matter how unsettled, chaotic and filled with conflict one's environment might be, one's being will remain peaceful and calm within the protection of the "Great Image." Within the journey of this life, the soul of the ordinary person stops when it comes upon beautiful music and delicious food rather than continuing the journey toward the Tao. In such a state of soul, if the Tao is spoken of, he will find it insipid and without flavor, and will not be attracted to it. Even if such a person looks upon the Tao, he will not know what reality he is really looking upon, and thus he will not consider It worthy of being seen. Thus, he will pass by this reality, and may even flee from It.

If such a person hears of the reality of the Tao, he will consider Its exposition to be unworthy to be heard. In the language of or-

55. Quran 3:103:

واعتصموا به حبل الله جميعا و لا تفرقوا

There is also a Persian proverb that states, "Be with God and live like a king, or be without God and do what you wish."

با خدا باش بادشاهي كن   بي خدا باش هرجه خواهي كن

dinary and forgetful man, he would not be in the mood to listen to the exposition of the reality of the Tao. He is unaware that if he attains the Tao and makes It the guiding principle of his action, he will realize that the Being, Power and Capability of the Tao have no limits and are inexhaustible.

******

Chapter Thirty-Six

Part I

Whenever (the Tao) wants to shrink something,
It expands it for some time.
Whenever It wants to weaken something, It strengthens it for some time.
Whenever It wants to abolish something, It exalts it for some time.
Whenever It wants to take away something, It gives it for some time.
This is what I would call "subtle wisdom."
The soft and weak overcome the hard and strong.

This chapter begins with several verses that present a Taoist clarification of the outward contradictions in this world, while at the same time indicating the profound meaning of these contradictions. Thus, Lao Tzu states that if the Tao wants to shrink something, before it becomes small the Tao temporarily expands it and makes it large. This verse and the three that follow largely pertain to the domain of human life and not nature, though in nature there are also some phenomena that possess such qualities.

Similarly, if the Tao wants to weaken something, first It temporarily makes it stronger. If It wants to abolish or destroy something, It will exalt it for a short while. All these actions of the Tao contain ethical lessons for human life, and the purpose of these verses is to bring one's attention to the ups and downs of life in this world, so that one does not become arrogant as a result of transient increase in status in different phases of life. Thus, Lao Tzu calls this "subtle wisdom," for since it is subtle it is not easily comprehended.

This part ends with the abiding teaching of the *Tao Te Ching* that in the end the subtle and the weak will prevail.

Part II

The fish must never leave the deep,
Likewise, the sharp weapons of the state must never be disclosed to men.

The fish in this verse are a symbol and metaphor for subtle wisdom and gnosis that must be kept hidden in the depth of one's being and awareness, and about which one must never be ostentatious. The sharp weapons of the state are a symbol for the sharp intellect, which must be hidden from ordinary people.

******

Chapter Thirty-Seven

Tao is permanently in the state of non-action;
yet It leaves nothing undone.
If lords and kings be able to abide by this (principle), the Ten Thousand Things will grow up and develop of their own accord.
However, if in the course of growth, they should desire to raise their heads (too high),
It would restrain them by the weight of the nameless uncarved block.
The nameless uncarved block will take them back to the (original) state of desirelessness.
And if (the people) become desireless and consequently tranquil, the whole world will become of its own accord peaceful.

The first verse of this chapter returns to the principle of non-action and the concept of *wu wei* that has been alluded to on several occasions previously. Without performing any action, that is, by observing the principle of non-action, the Tao accomplishes all acts.

If those who hold positions of authority and rule over society, the lords and kings, follow the example of the Tao and observe the principle of non-action rather than constantly interfering in all affairs, everyone will grow up and develop in a natural way. This growth, however, must be in accordance with both their nature and the reality of things. Otherwise, if they commit excess and go beyond their own limits, the Tao will restrain them with the uncarved block, which is a symbol of truth and reality itself.

By means of this very truth and reality, the uncarved block, which is also the principle of their very existence, the Tao will correct them and take them back to their natural state (in the Taoist sense of the term), which is freedom from the desires of the carnal soul. The purpose of this is ethical and religious cultivation, and if man achieves this goal and is freed from the desires of the carnal soul, all conflict and strife will end, and peace will prevail over the world.

******

BOOK TWO

Chapter Thirty-Eight

Part I

A man of superior virtue is not conscious of his virtue,
That is why he has virtue.
A man of inferior virtue tries hard not to lose his virtue,
That is why he is deprived of virtue.
A man of superior virtue keeps to non-action;
nor is he ever conscious of having done something.
A man of inferior virtue keeps to action, and is always conscious of having done something.
A man of superior benevolence acts, but is not conscious of having done something.
A man of superior righteousness acts, and is conscious of having done something.
A man of superior decorum acts, and if no one responds, he rolls up his sleeves and forces others (to follow the rules of decorum).

In the verses of this part, the *Tao Te Ching* presents a discussion of the hierarchy of virtues and how they are manifested in human beings. The first verse concerns the highest degree of virtue, stating that the one who truly possesses virtue considers it to be part of his very being, much like the faculties of seeing and hearing. He does not consciously regard virtue in the way that he regards pleasure or pain, for example, which occur for him but are not part of him and are thus seen as new and identifiable realities that have entered the domain of his being. By contrast, true virtue is intertwined with the being of the one who has made it deeply part of himself. Since such an individual does not see virtue in an artificial or extraneous way, he possesses virtue in the deepest and most authentic sense of the term, and naturally never boasts about it.

The second degree of virtue concerns one who, since he is not inherently virtuous, struggles consciously not to lose his virtue. Since his condition is as such he is deprived of virtue.

Lao Tzu returns to discuss the superior degree of virtue and repeats the principle that one who possesses the highest degree of virtue follows the principle of *wu wei* or non-action. He acts without acting, and as a result his action is natural, and he is not aware of his righteous actions in the sense of consciously directing his attention to them. Any action that arises from him is naturally accompanied by goodness and virtue.

In contrast, someone of inferior virtue accomplishes various actions and is always conscious of having done these deeds, which is to say that he does not accomplish good actions by nature but rather has to make effort in order to do so.

Likewise, an individual of superior benevolence, though accomplishing good deeds, does so according to his own nature, not with specific awareness that he is doing something good. However, an individual who possesses superior righteousness but has a particular intention in mind also acts, but is aware of this action and does not accomplish it naturally.

Lao tzu then also speaks of an individual whose principal quality is outward etiquette and decorum. Such an individual also acts and expects an appropriate response. If no one responds he will not sit quietly, but rather prepares himself to force others to be outwardly polite and to follow the external conventions of etiquette (that were common in Chinese society).

Part II

Thus it is only after the Tao is lost that virtue becomes prominent.
It is only after virtue is lost that benevolence becomes prominent.
It is only after benevolence is lost that righteousness becomes prominent.
It if only after righteousness is lost that the decorum becomes prominent.

In light of the above discussion, Lao Tzu concludes that it is only after the Tao is lost that the importance of virtue becomes evident, since so long as the Tao is present virtue is also present. When virtue is no longer present, benevolence becomes important. When benevolence is lost, righteousness, which is a double-edged sword that can lead one to self-righteousness, appears important. Finally, when righteousness is lost, etiquette and decorum, which here refer mainly to keeping up appearances, take its place.

Part III

Indeed, decorum indicates the scarcity of loyalty and good faith.

It marks the beginning of disorder.
Perspicacity is a flowery semblance of the Tao.
It marks the beginning of folly.
Therefore, the truly great man maintains himself on what is solid and thick not on what is thin and weak.
He keeps to the fruit and not the flower.
In fact, he rejects the latter and takes the former.

Formalities have existed in all societies including traditional Chinese society. However, from a spiritual point of view, their existence is a sign of the loss of the more profound virtues of loyalty and good faith. For example, for a Muslim performing the daily prayers is not a formality, but rather is accomplishing the Divine Command. Understanding this is the result of loyalty to God and faith in Him. If the daily prayers are reduced to a formality, they lose their inner meaning for the Muslim who performs them. If this happens, the result will be disorder on both the outward and inward levels, since loyalty to the covenant with the Origin and faith will have been lost.

Perspicacity (*baṣīrat*), in the sense of seeing things only in light of reason (*'aql-i juz'ī*, the particular intellect) and only witnessing the outward aspects of things (in contrast to the meaning of 'witnessing', *mushāhadah* in Islamic esoterism) has a superficial resemblance to the power of the Tao, but this resemblance has no depth and can be misleading. As Rūmī said,

"The particular intellect defamed the [Universal] Intellect."[56]

Whenever one relies on outward perspicacity alone, this is a sign of his ignorance and the beginning of his falling into the trap of folly. Thus, the one who is aware of the Truth, and is really a great man, stands firmly on the ground of the Truth, not on what is unsound and transitory. In comparison with truth, falsehood is always weak and unstable.

Such a man looks at the final fruits of action, not on the transitory stages that precede the final stage of things. He makes the final stage and the outcome of any action his goal, and not the stages of actions that have not yet yielded fruit.

******

56. Rūmī, *Mathnawī*, V:463.

عقل جزئی عقل را بدنام کرد   کام دنیا مرد را بی‌کام کرد

Chapter Thirty-Nine

Part I

Those that are from ancient times in possession of the One are the following:
Heaven, by virtue of the One, is serene.
Earth, by virtue of the One, is solid.
The spirits, by virtue of the One, exercise mysterious powers.
The valleys, by virtue of the One, are full.
The Ten Thousand Things, by virtue of the One, are alive.
The lords and kings, by virtue of the One, become the standard of the world.
It is the One that makes these beings what they are.

The first part of this chapter is devoted to Divine Unicity in a way that is profoundly similar to the Islamic conception, as when the Quran states, "Say, 'He, God, is One.'"[57] Thus, Lao Tzu states that from ancient times, which can be interpreted to mean "from the Origin," the realities mentioned in these verses possess the sign and imprint of Unicity, and not only the imprint of duality and organization around a single reality lower than the level of Unicity.

It is by virtue of the Grace of the One and its principle Attribute, which is Unicity, that Heaven is serene. And it is that same Grace of Unicity that has made the Earth solid and stable. And it is by virtue of that same Grace of Unicity that the world of spirits is possessed of mysterious powers and can and does exercise them. The valleys, which alludes to the domain of life of existents, including human beings, are filled with the Grace of Unicity. All beings, as alluded to by the words "the Ten Thousand Things," which indicates totality, are alive by virtue of the Grace of Unicity. And it is through the Grace of Unicity that those who gain the power of governance and kingship become standards for the world, that is, human society. And it is this very Blessing of Unicity that gives the rulers of the world the possibility to be what they are. So it is

57. Quran 112:1:

قُلْ هُوَ ٱللَّهُ أَحَدٌ

through the blessing of the manifestations of the Divine Truth, the One, that all aspects of existence are what they are.

Part II

If it were not for what makes it serene, Heaven would be rent in pieces.
If it were not for what makes it solid, the Earth would collapse.
If it were not for what makes them exercise mysterious powers,
the spirits would cease to be active.
If it were not for what makes them full, the valleys would run dry.
If it were not for what keeps them alive,
the Ten Thousand Things would perish.
If it were not for what keeps them in their high and noble position,
the lords and kings would be overthrown.

If that power that makes Heaven serene, namely the Grace of Unicity, did not exist, Heaven would not exist, or in other terms, "would be rent into pieces." Likewise, if the power that keeps the Earth firm and stable, namely the Grace of Unicity, did not exist, the Earth would collapse and cease to be. And if that power or Grace of Unicity that makes it possible for the spirits to exercise the mysterious powers given to them did not exist, they could no longer do anything and would cease to be active.

Similarly, if it were not for the Grace of Unicity, which permits the valleys to be full, that is, to provide the means of sustenance and activity for man and all other creatures, the valleys would run dry, which is to say that these activities would cease.

It is the Grace of Unicity that not only makes the existence of all beings possible but also keeps them alive. Thus, if it were not for this Grace of Unicity, or one could say Divine Emanation, all beings would cease to exist. And finally, if it were not for the Grace of Unicity, which is the ultimate cause of kings and rulers maintaining their high and noble positions, the rulers and wielders of authority and status in society would be overthrown.

Part III

Verily, the superior have the inferior as their roots,
and the high have the low as their bases.
This is why lords and kings refer to themselves as "the orphan," "the virtueless" and "the hapless." Is it not because they take the inferior as their roots? Is it not so?

Hence (it is said): Trying to acquire too many honors ends by acquiring no honor.
Do not be like shining jade. Be like coarse, unpolished stones.

The affairs of this world are based on hierarchies. The root, meaning the foundation, of higher levels is in the lower levels. This does not mean that the source of existence of beings of higher levels of existence is in the existence of lower levels. Rather, it means that the levels of existence are situated one above the other like the steps of a ladder.

In this way, the *Tao Te Ching* imparts an ethical lesson, stating that it is for this reason that the prominent members of society show themselves to be "orphans," "virtueless" and "hapless" to show that their power is based on the people following them. This is not to negate the importance of the Tao and the necessity of the rulers following it; for, as was mentioned previously, it is only through the assistance of the Tao that rulers can successfully govern over others.

Then Lao Tzu asks, is it not for this reason, that is, the existence of hierarchies in various respects, that people of prominence and authority rely on the people they govern? He draws the conclusion that, disregarding the importance of the relationship between levels within the hierarchy and one's relationship with others, and instead, making effort to gain honors for oneself, will result in failure to earn real honors altogether. Thus, Lao Tzu advises that one not try to shine like a jewel, but rather to be as a rough and unpolished stone, which means to be on a level of existence that is undetermined and unindividuated, an existence beyond this or that particular form.

******

Chapter Forty

Returning is how the Tao moves.
Being weak is how the Tao acts.
The Ten Thousand Things under Heaven are born out of Being
And Being is born out of Non-being.

This short chapter once again summarizes the reality of the Tao in a brief yet completely metaphysical way. The manner of "moving" or manifestation of the Tao is to return to the Principle and Origin, a characteristic that is also present existentially within human beings.

Whoever became distanced from his roots
Seeks to return to the days of his union.[58]

As has been discussed previously, from the Taoist perspective, being weak alludes to non-action within action, and not a lack of capability in the ordinary sense.

In the final two verses, Lao Tzu explains the foundation of metaphysics, that all beings originate from Being (*wujūd*), and Being itself originates from that Reality that is even beyond Being, which in the Chinese esoteric tradition is called "Non-being," not in the sense of lacking existence of being beneath it, but in the sense of the nameless and description-less Essence of the Divine Truth, which is even beyond Being. In some schools of Islamic philosophy, such as Ismā'īlī philosophy and certain other Islamic philosophical texts, this topic has been alluded to, and Being (*hastī* or *wujūd*) is itself considered the first delimitation that proceeds from the Essence of the Divine Truth.

******

58. Rūmī, *Mathnawī*, I:4.

هركسي كو دور ماند از اصل خويش　　باز جويد روزگار وصل خويش

Whoever becomes distanced from his roots
seeks to return to the days of his union.

Chapter Forty-One

Part I

When a man of the highest caliber hears about the Tao, he puts It into practice assiduously.
When a man of middle grade hears about the Tao, he appears to be half believing and half in doubt.
When a man of low grade hears about the Tao, he bursts into laughter.
If It is not laughed at, It would be not worthy of being the Tao.

Generally speaking, people can be classified into three groups: those who, if they encounter the truth, accept It and put It into practice; those who doubt the truth when they face It; and those who do not take the truth seriously and totally deny It. The verses in this chapter are devoted to a discussion of this subject, with the first verse stating that a man possessed of the highest caliber of character and comprehension of the truth, upon encountering the Tao, follows It and makes It the criterion of his action. As for one who belongs to the group below this and is halfhearted and unsure about the Tao, half of his being is in a state of belief and the other half is in doubt. This describes the condition of the majority of human beings in most aspects of life. Finally, when those who are totally unaware of the truth and occupy the lowest level of the human state hear about Ultimate Reality, the Tao, their reaction is to laugh at It and ridicule It.

This verse then adds a subtle yet important point that if an individual who is ignorant of the truth does not ridicule something, then it is not worthy of being called the Tao. In reality, the negation of the truth by an ignorant person is itself an indication of the fact that what he denies is the truth of the Tao.

Part II

An old traditional saying has it:
"A way that is bright appears dark.
A way that goes straight ahead seems to go backward.
The way that is flat and even appears rough and rugged.

Chapter Forty-One

The highest virtue looks like the valley.
The purest white appears sullied.
The widest virtue appears insufficient.
The strongest virtue appears feeble.
The simplest and purest color appears faded.
The greatest square has (apparently) no corners.
The greatest vessel appears un-completed.
The loudest sound is scarcely audible.
The greatest form is formless."
The Tao is hidden and has no name.
Yet, it is the Tao alone that really excels in bestowing help and bringing all things to completion.

In this part, the *Tao Te Ching* refers to a Chinese proverb that explains profound realities through allusion to their opposites. As such, Lao Tzu states that even though the path toward the Divine Truth is essentially bright and luminous, it looks dark for the one who has never traversed this path. In Sufi discussions of spiritual wayfaring, it is likewise mentioned that in the beginning of the journey, the realities of this world appear bright and real, and the realities of the celestial realm appear dark, invisible, and incomprehensible. However, as the traveler advances in wayfaring, it becomes clear to him that in reality it is this world that is dark and the realities of the celestial realm are incandescent and luminous.

Similarly, Lao Tzu warns that when traversing "the way that goes ahead," that is, the straight path, it may appear to the wayfarer as if he is moving backward. This issue is also discussed in the teachings of Sufism as well.

The path toward the Truth is flat, but for an imperfect individual it is filled with ups and downs. Here Lao Tzu once again refers to the symbol of the lowness of a valley, which although being low is filled with bounties and blessings, and as such virtue is similar to a valley.

In the same way, something extremely white appears to be sullied. In life, certain matters arise in which the strongest virtues appear weak and feeble. This same phenomenon of the reversal of meanings is also true of colors, as a pure color often looks colorless. This apparent contradiction can be observed in all other domains of reality. If a geometric form such as a square is extremely large, its corners cannot be seen, as if it were a square without any corners. Likewise, the completeness of an extremely large vessel will not be visible, and hence it will seem incomplete. Similarly, a very loud sound is almost inaudible.

Finally, this part returns to the principle of the Tao, that it is the greatest form and yet is formless. In the Quran it is stated that, "wheresoever you turn, there is the Face of God,"[59] even though God's "Face" or "Form" (*ṣūrat*) has no form.[60] This best of all forms, the "form" of the Tao, is hidden from the outward eye, and although it is called the Tao, It is nameless, that is, It is beyond all forms of delimitation.

Indeed, the Tao has no name, yet nonetheless It is a Reality that excels in bringing about the possibility for accomplishing all things and bringing them to completion, which is to say that It is the True Actor and the Supreme Cause.

******

---

59. Quran 2:115:
وَلِلَّهِ الْمَشْرِقُ وَالْمَغْرِبُ فَأَيْنَمَا تُوَلُّوا فَثَمَّ وَجْهُ اللَّهِ إِنَّ اللَّهَ وَاسِعٌ عَلِيم

60. Here the Persian commentary makes use of the fact that in Persian the word *ṣūrat* means both "form" and "face."

Chapter Forty-Two

Part I

Tao begets One.
One begets Two.
Two begets Three.
And three begets the Ten Thousand Things.
The Ten Thousand Things carry on their backs the yin and embrace in their arms the yang. And the two are kept in harmonious union by the (third) energy emerging out of them.

The first part of this chapter reaffirms the foundational principles of Taoist philosophy. The Tao is the Absolute Origin, corresponding to the Essence of God, and from It the first emanation (*fayḍ wa ṣudūr*) is the One. This first emanation is itself one because the Tao is one [as it is said], "from one nothing issues except one."[61] In Chinese philosophy, the One that issues from the Tao is Being, before the actualization of all the potentialities that it contains.

The first emanation from the Tao is Itself in turn the source of the emanation of Two, or duality, which is precisely yin and yang. From Two in turn issues Three or trinity, which is actually a manner of return to unity, as is also found in the Pythagorean philosophy of arithmetic, in the *Epistles of the Brethren of Purity* and other Islamic sources.[62] While two is a step toward separation, three is a return to oneness.

Finally, Three is the origin of multiplicity, or in the terms of

61. On this key philosophical principle, see Davlat Dadikhuda, "Rule of the One: Avicenna, Bahmanyār, and al-Rāzī on the Argument from the *Mubāḥathāt*," *Nazariyat* 6, no. 2 (2020): 69–97. For a typical theological criticism of it, see Abū Ḥāmid al-Ghazzāli, *The Incoherence of the Philosophers*, ed. and trans. Michael E. Marmura (Provo: Brigham Young University Press, 2000), 65ff; ʿAyn al-Quḍāt, *The Essence of Reality: A Defense of Philosophical Sufism*, trans. Mohammed Rustom (New York: NYU Press, 2023), chapter 39 and 60.

62. On the *Brethren of Purity* (*Ikhwān al-Ṣafā'*) see Nader El-Bizri (ed.), *The Ikhwân al-Safâ' and their Rasâ'il*, New York: Oxford University Press in Association with the Institute of Ismaili Studies, 2008. See also, G. de Callatay, *Ikhwân al-Safa'. A Brotherhood of Idealists on the Fringe of Orthodox Islam*, Oxford: Oneworld, 2005.

Chinese philosophy "the Ten Thousand Things." Notwithstanding minor differences, this schema of the degrees of being in the *Tao Te Ching* is very much comparable to the five Divine Presences articulated by Ibn 'Arabī and other Muslim sages.

Lao Tzu adds that all things existing in the world (the Ten Thousand Things) possess yin and yang. Carrying yin on their back and embracing yang in their arms, they are kept united and harmonious by a third factor, an energy that issues from both yin and yang.

Part II

Ordinary men detest more than anything else being an "orphan," "virtueless" and "hapless."
Yet, kings and lords use these terms in referring to themselves.
This shows that a thing is sometimes increased by being diminished and diminished by being increased.
What others teach, I also teach, namely: "A daring and violent man will not die a natural death." I regard this as the father of all precepts.

The ordinary human being does not want to be orphaned, alone, virtueless and helpless, and detests these conditions. Yet it is strange that despite this, kings and dignitaries use these same attributes for themselves. From the gnostic and philosophical point of view, this is a kind of pretension that brings them social and political benefit.

The *Tao Te Ching* considers this fact an indication of the universal truth that in some situations something may increase by being diminished and diminish by being increased. One domain in which this principle can be seen is human behavior. Humility and modesty make one great, while arrogance, pride, and self-aggrandizement humiliate one and diminish one's value.

Lao Tzu indicates that the lesson he is giving is the same which others, that is, the time-honored Chinese tradition, has imparted, namely that a daring and oppressive individual "does not die a natural death," meaning that in the end he will perish as a result of this constant strife and conflict rather than by natural causes.

******

Chapter Forty-Three

The softest of all things in the world dominates over the hardest of all things in the world.
Having no definite form of its own, it penetrates even into that which has no crevices. By this I realize the value of non-action.
Teaching without words, and the effect of non-action, few in the world can equal them.

This short chapter presents another expression of Taoist philosophy concerning the significance of *wu wei* or non-action. In contrast to what ordinary people suppose, it states that the softest things dominate over the hardest things. This principle can be observed in water, which is soft, dripping on stone, which is hard. The drops of this soft water will eventually create a hole in the hard stone.

The softest things do not have a particular form of their own, just like water, which always takes the form of the container into which it is poured. Yet, this formless thing enters into even those things that have no cracks or crevices, again like water dripping on stone. Lao Tzu states that from this simple example he realizes an important truth, namely the value of acting without acting or "non-action," *wu wei*. By indicating this, he wishes us also to attend to this truth.

Only the sages and a selected few comprehend teaching without words and the possibility of acting without acting and put them into practice. Understanding this truth is not possible for everyone.

******

Chapter Forty-Four

Your fame or your Self - which is dearer to you?
Your Self or your wealth - which is more valuable to you?
Gain or loss - which is more baneful to you?
Therefore, excessive stinginess is sure to lead to great waste.
Amassing too much wealth is sure to end in heavy loss.
If you know contentment, you will suffer no humiliation.
If you know where to stop, you will meet with no danger.
You will then remain forever safe.

The ordinary person is constantly in search of fame and recognition. Lao Tzu asks us a philosophical question: which is dearer - personal, individualistic fame or one's Self, which indicates the innermost Center of one's being and which is precisely the Tao, and which is none other than the Divine Reality, which according to Muslim gnostics is the very Self or Essence residing in the heart of the being of the human?

He then asks another question of all people: which is more valuable, that Self, which is the principle of your being, or the wealth that you amass and that gives you a sense of self-worth? Is accumulating more wealth more harmful or losing it and having nothing? In various commentaries on this chapter, "gain" and "loss" have been interpreted in different ways, from indicating gain or loss of material wealth, or gaining or losing access to the Divine Essence within the human heart, or acquiring or losing fame in society. Lao Tzu concludes that excessive stinginess will undoubtedly result in waste of what one has acquired. Likewise, excessive amassing of wealth will ultimately end in heavy loss.

As was indicated previously, if man is content with what he has and is not excessive, he will not be subject to humiliation by others. As is also discussed in Islamic ethics, one who trusts God and is content with that which pleases God will be protected from being humiliated by others.

One of the most important ethical lessons is to know one's limits and where to stop in each matter. If one has this awareness and is not excessive, one will not confront many dangers and will be safe from them. Such an individual is always safe and in peace. In the teachings of Islam this truth can be seen in the etymological connection between the terms *amān*, meaning security and well-being, and *īmān*, meaning faith. He who possesses true faith is always in peace and safety.

******

Chapter Forty-Five

The greatest perfection seems imperfect; yet when used,
it will never wear out.
The greatest fullness seems empty; yet when used,
it will never be exhausted.
The greatest straightness seems twisted.
The greatest dexterity seems awkward.
The greatest eloquence seems stammering.
Restless movement overcomes coldness.
But it is quietness that overcomes heat.
That which is serene and quiet becomes the norm of all under Heaven.

He who possesses the greatest perfection is free from pretentiousness regarding perfection, and thus to the eye that sees, only the outward seems to lack perfection. However, since he possesses true perfection, no matter how often his thoughts and words are made use of, they will not lose their perfection and will never wear out.

A container that is completely full may look empty, but since it is truly full, however much of its content is used, more will yet remain and it will not be exhausted. This principle is illustrated by the use of the word "full" (*pur*) in Persian for someone who is truly knowledgeable. However much such an individual uses his knowledge, he remains knowledgeable and will not be emptied of knowledge.

The third verse pertains more to the human realm and domain of thought than to the material world. For example, a straight road does not appear twisted, but shows itself as straight. In the case of man, however, the truthfulness of an individual and his thoughts on the highest level will seem complicated or twisted to one who lacks truth, just as for the followers of an agnostic philosophy or one who denies Absolute Reality, the perspective of those who speak of the Truth appears obscure and twisted.

One who is truly skilled at something, does it so easily, and often so quickly, that to those who only see the outward, his skill does not match the task assigned to him. This fact has been discussed in many Islamic mystical and ethical texts in many different ways.

True eloquence and mastery of a language is accompanied by fluency and lucidity of expression, and is never overcomplicated. Thus, one who sees only the outward, mistakes it for being shallow and stammering.

It is natural for a person who feels cold to overcome the coldness he experiences with restless (which is to say fast and continuous) movement. This is not limited to the sensory world (*'ālam-i maḥsūsāt*), but also applies to the realm of thought and the psyche. However, in this realm movement must be accompanied by order and meaning, rather than being chaotic, otherwise one's thought will remain "cold," meaning unfruitful and inconsequential.

In contrast, it is peace and serenity that will overcome heat. Here "heat" signifies movement and action accompanied by tension, anxiety, and directionless and fruitless effort, which must be overcome by the peace of the Spirit.

He who can attain inner peace, whether intellectual or emotional, is the criterion of perfection not only for other human beings but for all beings in this world, or in the words of the text, "all under Heaven."

******

Chapter Forty-Six

Part I

When Tao prevails in the world, swift horses are sent back
to be used for plowing the fields.
When Tao does not prevail in the world, war horses are bred
in the vicinity of the city walls.

The two verses in this part of the chapter show the contradictory consequences of applying and not applying the Tao in the human domain. In cases in which the Tao governs the human world, there is no need for swift horses for either war or traveling hastily, since everything unfolds calmly according to the principles of the Tao. As a result, these horses are used for agriculture.

However, if society is such that the Tao does not prevail, things will not be in their right places, such that even warhorses, which should be in the battlefield, are kept and bred beside the city walls. That is to say, they are not where they are supposed to be.

Part II

There is no crime greater than giving reign to desires.
There is no calamity greater than not knowing how to be content.
There is no fault greater than being covetous.
Therefore, he who knows how to be content and remains content
will always remain content.

This part deals with ethics and the negativity of the vices, stating that the greatest crime is for one not to be in control over the "soul that incites to ugliness" (*al-nafs al-ammarah bi'l-su'*) and its desires and to set it free. In traditional thought the objective is not freedom *of* the carnal soul but freedom *from* it.

To know how to attain the spiritual station of contentment consists of a great blessing for the human spirit. There is no calamity and affliction greater than not knowing how to attain this station.

Covetousness is one of the major faults of the ordinary human soul and there is no greater defect. One must be careful not to allow covetousness to increase.

From these pieces of ethical advice Lao Tzu concludes that we must learn how to be always content and satisfied. He who reaches a station in which he can comprehend the reality of contentment and in which these qualities become part of his very being will always be content and satisfied, and these virtues will never abandon him.

******

Chapter Forty-Seven

Without going out of the door, one can know everything under Heaven.
Without peeping out of the window, one can have a view
of the working of Heaven.
The further one goes out, the less one knows.
Therefore, the sage knows without going out.
He has a clear view of everything without looking.
He accomplishes everything without acting.

The entirety of this chapter concerns the inner world, which, being the microcosm, contains all the realities of the outside world. Thus it states that without even traveling in the outside world man can know everything that exists under heaven. The realities of the objective world are all within man, as Christ said, "The Kingdom of God is within you." Self-knowledge is the key to knowledge of God, and knowledge of God may also include knowledge of His creation. The journey of the soul (*sayr-i anfus*) in one sense also encompasses the journey on the horizons (*sayr-i āfāq*).[63] It is in light of this truth that our gnostics (*'urafā*) consider the journey to the heart to be the way to reach the Beloved.

O people who have gone to make the Ḥajj,
Where are you? Where are you?
The Beloved is right here.
Come here! Come here![64]

So a sage can gain awareness of the workings of Heaven without even looking outside, without this statement negating the objective reality of Heaven's activity. The more one is outward looking, the less he will attain true wisdom, unless he looks outward *after* attaining gnosis of the realities within, as a result of which he will

63. An allusion to Quran 41:53: "We shall show them Our signs upon the horizons and within themselves till it becomes clear to them that it is the truth."
سَنُرِيهِمْ آيَاتِنَا فِي الْآفَاقِ وَفِي أَنفُسِهِمْ حَتَّىٰ يَتَبَيَّنَ لَهُمْ أَنَّهُ الْحَقُّ

64. Rūmī, *Divān-i Kabīr, Ghazal* no. 648, Tehran, 13th ed. 1372/1993, p. 274.
اي قوم به حج رفته كجاييد   معشوق همينجاست بياييد بياييد

witness the realities within him in the external world. The result of these truths is that the sage succeeds in attaining gnosis without the help of experience of the external world.

By attaining inward gnosis, the sage gains a clear vision of the realities of all things without the need to look at them. He is fully aware of the correspondence between inward realities and the realities of the objective world, and it is this correspondence that illuminates why and how gnosis of the external world is possible without outward experience.

The result of this gnosis is that the sage accomplishes everything without acting, that is, by attaining a spiritual station governed by *wu wei*.

******

Chapter Forty-Eight

If one pursues learning, (knowledge) increases day by day.
If one pursues Tao, (knowledge) decreases day by day.
Decreasing, and ever more decreasing, one finally reaches
the state of non-action.
Once one has reached the state of non-action, nothing is left undone.
Even an empire is gained by practicing (the simplicity of)
"there-is-nothing-to-do."
If one adheres to (the principle of) "there-is-something-to-do,"
one can never gain an empire.

While the previous chapter was concerned with inward gnosis, this chapter deals with outward and exoteric knowledge and its contrast to inner wisdom. Thus, Lao Tzu states that if one's objective is to acquire knowledge in the ordinary sense of the term, which is to say outward knowledge, naturally this knowledge will increase for him day by day. The verse indirectly suggests that such a path will not lead one closer to the Tao. This type of outward knowledge stands in contrast to gnosis of the Tao. For one who seeks the Tao, the thirst to acquire formal knowledge, rather than increasing, in fact decreases day by day. His objective is to attain unity, rather than to immerse himself ever more in multiplicity and knowledge of multiplicity. This is the way a true seeker seeks.

See one, say one, know one,
For through this, the root and branches of faith are sealed.[65]

For the Taoist sage the thirst to acquire knowledge of the world of multiplicity decreases constantly until he reaches the station of non-action or *wu-wei*. For the one who attains this station there is nothing else left to accomplish. This principle even applies in the realm of politics, and by means of it one can gain an empire. By contrast, if one does not put this truth into practice, from the Taoist point of view, he can never possess an empire, even though

65. Maḥmūd Shabastarī, *The Rose Garden of Divine Mysteries: Gulshan-i rāz*, op. cit.
یکی بین و یکی گوی و یکی دان بدین ختم آمد اصل و فرع ایمان

one may possess many other virtues and abilities. One must bear in mind that this is a Taoist teaching and not that of Confucianism, the teachings of which are also fundamental for understanding the totality of traditional Chinese civilization.

******

Chapter Forty-Nine

The sage has no fixed mind of his own.
He makes the mind of all people his mind.
"Those who are good, I treat as good.
But those who are not good, also I treat as good.
For the original nature of man is goodness."
"Those who are faithful I treat as faithful.
But even those who are not faithful l also treat as faithful.
For the original nature of man is faithfulness."
The sage, while in this world, cautiously keeps his mind confused and obscure for the sake of the world.
The ordinary people strain their eyes and ears.
The sage keeps his eyes and ears (free) like an infant.

The Taoist sage does not have a dogmatic and rigid mind that is closed to diverse truths. This of course does not mean that he is not permanently attached to the Tao, to which his being is always connected. He is a freethinker in the true sense of the term, and the doors of his mind are open to the outside. However, it must not be forgotten that the walls of his mind remain intact. If a room does not have walls, it does not matter if its doors and windows are open or closed. This is a metaphor for being openminded or enlightened (*rawshan-fikrī*) in the ordinary sense of the term. Since the doors of the mind of a sage are open, he allows the thought of others to enter his mind, investigates and assesses it and considers it his own.

In the next few verses, a monologue of such a sage is presented, explaining his behavior. He states that he treats those who are good with goodness, and adds this important ethical teaching that he also treats those who are not good with goodness.

The comfort of this world and the next
is summarized in two words,
Chivalry with friends, and tolerance with the foes.[66]

66. Ḥāfiẓ, op. cit., p. 5.
آسایش دوگیتی تفسیر این دو حرف است   با دوستان مروت با دشمنان مدارا

The reason the sage behaves like this is that he believes human nature is good, just as human nature is believed to be essentially good in Sufism. Since "man is born upon the primordial nature (*fiṭrah*),"[67] not only does the sage consider his own nature in relation to others, he is always aware that this eternal nature is also within others, whether they appear to act well or badly.

The sage then turns to the important virtue of faithfulness, stating that he acts faithfully with those who are faithful. Again, he adds an important ethical teaching in that he is faithful towards those who are unfaithful. This is exceedingly difficult for ordinary people, and it is only a sage who can act in this way. The Sufis see this to be a quality of true lovers, who are loyal even if they see the beloved as disloyal. The Taoist sage then reiterates that this attitude is rooted in the fact that faithfulness is one of the attributes of the human primordial nature.

As long as the sage lives in this world, he keeps his mind "confused and obscure" which here means that he keeps his mind open so that he can assess everything free of discrimination and prejudice. Ordinary people "strain their eyes and ears" in order to keep their prejudice and discrimination against others. By contrast, the eyes and ears of a sage are like those of a child, meaning that they are in an ideal state of unity before the manifestation of otherness and the separation resulting from contraries.

******

67. Ḥadīth, Saḥīḥ al-Bukhārī #4775.
ما من مولود الا يولد على الفطرة

Chapter Fifty

When one way leads to life while the other leads to death, three out of ten take the way of life, three out of ten take the way of death, and three out of ten are those who want to remain alive but by bustling about, betake themselves of their own accord to the realm of death.
Why is that so? Because they pursue life too assiduously.
I have heard it said that one who excels in maintaining his life does not meet with rhinoceros and tigers when traveling on land nor is he wounded by weapons when he goes into battle.
There is no place in his body for a rhinoceros to drive its horn.
There is no place for the tiger to put its claws.
There is no place for the sword to thrust its blade.
Why is this so? Because in him there is no death-spot.

Human beings, in accordance with their nature and nurture, as well as the situations in which they find themselves, choose different paths. As such, Lao Tzu classifies people into three groups, calling each "three out of ten," by which a third is meant. If people are faced with a fork in the road where one way ends in death and the other life, one third, or as the text has it, three in ten will choose the way of life. Three in ten will choose the way of death, although perhaps what is meant here is not intentionally choosing a way that leads to death, but rather unwittingly taking such a path. Finally, one third wish to choose a path that leads to the continuation of their lives, yet as a result of pointless struggling and fruitless activity, they head towards death of their own accord. Without it being explicitly mentioned, it is implied in this categorization that the third group are unable to differentiate between effective and pointless effort, and as a result of their noisy but empty bustling, they are drawn towards the valley of death.

Lao Tzu then asks why this is so, and answers that it is because the third group struggles excessively, like someone who falls into a swamp- the more he struggles, the deeper he goes. Such struggle must not be mistaken for true effort in the positive sense of the term.

Lao Tzu then presents an important point regarding caution to our attention in an allegorical manner. He explains that he who has the wisdom to excel in maintaining and defending his life will travel in a manner that avoids danger, such that he does not encounter wild animals such as tigers and rhinoceroses. Even if he goes to war, he acts in such a way that he is not wounded by the weapons that he faces. His body has no point of weakness for a rhinoceros to drive its horn, and there is no place on his body that a sword can enter. These two verses allude to the fact that the perfect man does not have any weak point by which he can be harmed.

Again, Lao Tzu asks why this is so, answering that the sage has gone beyond death and hence cannot be slain. This statement directly alludes to the soul that has acquired virtue and clings to the Tao, in whose being the Tao flows.

******

Chapter Fifty-One

The Tao gives birth to all things, the Virtue fosters them, the "things" furnish them with definite forms, and the natural impetus completes their development.
That is why there is none of the Ten Thousand Things that does not venerate the Tao nor honor the Virtue.
The Tao is venerated and the Virtue esteemed not because it is commanded by somebody, but because they are naturally so.
Thus the Tao gives birth to all things and the Virtue fosters them.
It makes them grow, nourishes them, gives definite forms to them, provides them with special qualities, rears them, and shelters them.
It gives them life, yet claims no possession.
It does great things, yet does not boast of them.
It makes them grow, yet exercises no authority over them.
This is what I call the mysterious Virtue.

As was mentioned previously in this book, the Tao is the origin of existence; all things issue from It or, in the words of the text, are born from It. After this first level of reality (namely the Tao, the effect of which is to give life to all existing things), it is Virtue that encompasses them; nurturing and fostering them falls within its authority. On the next level, existents acquire their forms, gaining particular existence and becoming "things." Finally, the natural force within things guides them toward the perfection that accords with their nature, and ultimately perfects them. This fourfold division of the existentiation of things, namely the Tao, Virtue, things, and their natural impetus, is very similar to the four ontological levels of Neoplatonism, that is, the One, the Intellect, the Soul, and Nature, which were also well known to Muslim philosophers.

The "Ten Thousand Things" are born of these phases of emanation of existence, and thus intrinsically accept them, venerate the Tao, and honor Virtue. Such veneration is an essential reality, and if among the Ten Thousand Things there are some human beings who are negligent of this truth, it is because they are negligent of their own reality as a result of the freedom that has been granted to them. They have forgotten their own selfhood, whereas all other beings possess this awareness essentially and in accordance with their ontological reality and do not have the freedom to forget it.

Veneration of the Tao and honoring Virtue is not the effect of external pressure or compulsion. Rather, the nature of the Tao and Virtue is such that veneration of them is natural and ontological, and is a result of their very substance, not the command of anyone. To emphasize this, Lao Tzu reminds the reader that first the Tao brings all things into existence and then Virtue nurtures and cultivates them.

The subject of the remaining verses of this chapter is the Tao, though as It is assisted by Virtue. Thus it is that the Tao oversees all the stages of the existence of beings, from growth and nutrition to the bestowal of a particular form to each of them and qualities appropriate to their mode of being, as well as bringing them to maturity and even providing them with shelter, which here denotes not only a human dwelling but rather shelter for all existents.

It is the Tao Itself that gives life, but despite this gift and the gift of everything described above, the Tao Itself does not claim to possess them. "Possession" here is used in the ordinary sense of the term, and not in the sense of ontological possession, which is also mentioned in the Quran.[68] In a matter that is completely Taoist, Lao Tzu again states that the Tao accomplishes great things but does not boast of its positive actions in the way humans do. Again, this must not be mistaken with the belief in Divine Grandeur (*kibriyā*) in Islamic thought.

Similarly, the Tao is a power that nurtures everything yet does not display Its authority, especially to human beings who have been left free to find the way to gain awareness of the authority of the Tao. The *Tao Te Ching* calls this reality "the mysterious Virtue." The Virtue of the Tao is mysterious precisely because it is not accompanied with pretentiousness, is generally not noticed by ordinary people, and cannot be witnessed with the outward-seeing eye, despite its ontological effects being everywhere.

> Gaze upon the inner dimension of the world
> with the eye of inwardness,
> For with outward eye,
> thou shalt not see the inward.[69]

---

68. See for example, Quran 2:284:
لِّلَّهِ مَا فِى ٱلسَّمَـٰوَٰتِ وَمَا فِى ٱلْأَرْضِ ۗ وَإِن تُبْدُوا۟ مَا فِىٓ أَنفُسِكُمْ أَوْ تُخْفُوهُ يُحَاسِبْكُم بِهِ ٱللَّهُ ۖ فَيَغْفِرُ لِمَن يَشَآءُ
وَيُعَذِّبُ مَن يَشَآءُ ۗ وَٱللَّهُ عَلَىٰ كُلِّ شَىْءٍ قَدِيرٌ

69. Nāṣir Khusraw, op. cit., p. 66. Translation is taken from S.H. Nasr, *Religion and the Order of Nature*, New York & Oxford: Oxford University Press, 1996, p. 17.

Chapter Fifty-Two

Part I

All things under Heaven have a beginning which is to be regarded as the Mother of the Ten Thousand Things.
If you know the Mother, you know the Child. And if, after having known the Child, you go back to the Mother, and hold fast to Her, you will never fall into danger till the end of your life.

Here Lao Tzu refers to the beginning of the world as "the Mother." This is to some extent similar to the philosophical interpretation of the saying in Islam that paradise or the celestial world, which contains the archetype of the existence of this world, is under the feet of mothers. Lao Tzu then states that one can consider all creatures of the world, the Ten Thousand Things, to be born of that "Mother."

As a result, if one can know that "Mother," one can know her "Child" also. In philosophical language, by possessing the root or principle one can gain awareness of the branch or application, which is similar to the Platonic teaching on the world of forms and its manifestations in the world.

However, there is also a complementary approach, which is to know the "Child," through which one can become aware of the reality of the "Mother." This perspective is similar to Aristotelian teachings. Here Lao Tzu makes an important addition to this expression: if one is able to reach the "Mother" through the "Child" and cling on to Her, he will never face danger in life, since from the perspective of the spiritual world he has been freed from the world that contains danger.

Part II

Block the openings, shut the doors, and all your life you will not be exhausted.
If on the contrary, you unblock the openings and increase their activities, till the end of your life you will not be saved.
To be able to perceive the minutest things is what I would call illumination.

To be able to hold fast to weakness is strength.
If, using your external light, you go back to your internal illumination, you will never bring misfortune upon yourself.
Such a state I would call stepping into the Eternal.

After explaining these realities, Lao Tzu presents a series of instructions: he commands [the reader] to "block the openings," indicating that one should close the gates of the five senses that open to the outside world in order to be freed from the world of forms. He also advises us to "shut the doors," meaning to find freedom from the constant and uncultivated activity of the mind, which always moves from one concept to another, and from the various thoughts that arise until one has gained control of them. Until one does this, the passing of life will be exhausting. However, if one does close the openings and doors, one will not become exhausted, and life will not wear one out.

Doing the opposite of these instructions will lead to the inverse result: if one opens the doors to the outside and each day becomes more and more involved in outward activity, one will not be saved from instability and dispersion so long as one lives.

"To be able to perceive the minutest things" means to be able to apprehend realities that cannot be reached through the outward senses and are beyond their ability to provide knowledge. Lao Tzu calls this perception of "the minutest things" illumination (*ishrāq*). In a completely Taoist manner, he adds that taking recourse and holding fast to that which is seemingly soft and weak (but in reality is the principle of all existents) is precisely power and not weakness. Spiritual power is in the ability to know the inner reality of phenomena and not their outward appearances, however much that inner reality may seem weak and powerless to the superficial gaze.

"External light" denotes knowledge acquired through the outward senses, as was discussed above. If one can go back from this type of knowledge to the illumination of the intellect and spirit within, he will not bring upon himself misery and misfortune in the true sense of the term, meaning that he will remain ever fortunate and happy. True happiness is grounded in the inner journey and attaining the spiritual realm. Otherwise, it is outward and transient.

Attaining such true happiness is so fundamental and permanent that Lao Tzu considers it to be entering the station of eternity and everlastingness.

******

Chapter Fifty-Three

Part I

If I happen to be in possession of even a modicum of knowledge, I would be in grave danger of going astray even if I am actually walking on the main road.
The main road is level and safe; yet men tend to choose narrow sideways.

He who possesses only a modicum of the power of intellectual discernment is in danger of deviating from the right way, even if he is traveling on the straight path, even though he may walk on the straight path. It is in light of this reality that Muslims repeat the verse "Guide us upon the Straight Path" in every cycle of the daily prayers from the time they reach adulthood until the end of their lives.[70] This is because at every step one may deviate from the Straight Path, and hence it is always necessary to repeat this verse.

The "main road," which is precisely the Straight Path, is always level and safe. However, fallen man possesses a carnal soul that instigates him to deviate from the main road and to go astray, or in the words of the text, "to choose narrow sideways." It is in the nature of the carnal soul, which "commands to evil," to drive one to these "narrow sideways."[71]

Part II

The government offices are kept very clean, but the fields are
desolate and the granaries are empty.
Yet, there are people beautifully dressed carrying sharp swords at their sides, satiated with food and drink, and possessed of redundant wealth.
This is what I would call the luxury life of robbers.
This is indeed a deviation from the Tao.

After explaining these principles, this part turns to the domains of

70. Quran 1:6:

اهْدِنَا الصِّرَاطَ الْمُسْتَقِيمَ

71. Quran 12:53: "Surely the [carnal] soul commands to evil."

إِنَّ النَّفْسَ لَأَمَّارَةٌ بِالسُّوءِ

politics and government with a critical eye. Lao Tzu reproachfully states that, when governments are not run in accordance with Taoist principles, proper appearances are always well maintained and centers of power are kept clean while the affairs of the society are not attended to. As a result, fields are not irrigated properly and consequently there is no harvest to fill the granaries, so they remain empty. The people suffer while the ruling elites live in prosperity and abundance.

Those who govern society wear fine clothes and carry with them sharp swords, which symbolize their power. They have access to the best food and drink and amass enormous wealth for themselves.

Lao Tzu is strongly opposed to this lifestyle and criticizes it with the harshest possible language, calling it "the luxury life of robbers." Here we must bear in mind that simplicity in life has always been the ideal of the Taoist tradition, and in the history of China Taoist sages, following the teachings of Lao Tzu, have always been critical of the luxurious lifestyle.

******

Chapter Fifty-Four

Part I

What is firmly planted cannot be pulled out.
What is tightly embraced will not slip out.
This is (the principle) by which the ancestral sacrifice by the descendants will be kept uninterrupted forever.

The word "what" in the first two verses alludes to the virtue of the Tao, which must be "planted" deeply in one's being so that it remains here and guides one to perfection. If this is done in a profound rather than a shallow way, It will stay in one's spirit and soul forever and cannot be removed, in the same way that a spiritual station (*maqām*) in the spiritual wayfaring of Sufism is permanent, whereas a spiritual state (*ḥāl*) is transient.

The second verse explains the same truth in a different language: if man tightly embraces the virtue of the Tao, this reality will remain within him forever and will not disappear. The words "slip out" here do not imply freedom but rather loss.

To perform sacrifices for one's ancestors is one of the most important religious rituals in China. Lao Tzu states that it is because of and by way of, the presence of the virtue of the Tao in people that the ritual of sacrifice for the ancestors will continue forever without disruption.

Part II

If one cultivates it in one's own person, its effect will be genuine (in the person).
If one cultivates it in the family, its effect will be more than sufficient (in the family).
If one cultivates it in the village, its effect will last long (in the village).
If one cultivates it in the state, its effect will be abundant (in the state).
If one cultivates it in the world, its effect will be universal.

The second part of this chapter discusses the entire spectrum of the effects of planting the virtue of the Tao in the depths of the soul of the individual and his society. This spectrum begins with man himself and then extends to other domains of this world. As such, Lao Tzu states that if one preserves and cultivates "it," meaning the virtue of the Tao, in oneself, its effects will remain in one's being in a genuine way.

If one inculcates this reality in one's own family, which is the foundation of society, its effects will be even more than one would expect. Beyond the family, it is one's social group that is most important in terms of daily experience in the traditional world, and this can also be extended to one's district within a city. Here again, the cultivation of this reality is not temporary, but will remain for a long time. Similarly, if this reality spreads throughout the state, it will have a profound impact upon that state. Finally, if people are able to inculcate this reality throughout the world, that is, beyond the borders of China, its effects will also be global and will not be limited only to the borders of China and the domain of the Taoist tradition. Genuine religions are such that even if they were revealed for a specific group of people, they nevertheless contain a universal message within themselves.

Part III

Thus by looking at a person, you can rightly estimate the person.
By looking at a family, you can rightly estimate the family.
By looking at a village, you can rightly estimate the village.
By looking at a state, you can rightly estimate the state.
By looking at the whole world, you can rightly estimate the whole world.
How do I know that the world is like this? By means of what I have just said.

After discussing the criterion for the assessment of various individual and social realities, Lao Tzu addresses the individual who has attained the origin of the degrees of perfection and affirms that in such an individual there is sufficient knowledge to assess the state of a family by examining it in a correct and profound way.

The same holds true for a village or the close social group that surrounds one, just as it is applicable to a state. Through studying a state, a perfected individual can assess the condition of that state accurately. Finally, this principle also applies to the entire world.

This indicates that to have correct views one is not limited to one's own culture and society, but rather it is possible to evaluate the world and hold a worldview that is universal.

Lao Tzu concludes this chapter with an allusion, posing the question: How does he know that such is the reality of the world? His response is that he has provided the answer in what was mentioned above, and hence we must refer to what was expressed earlier in order to find it.

******

Chapter Fifty-Five

Part I

He who contains within himself the plenitude of the Virtue
may be compared to an infant.
Poisonous snakes do not bite it.
Ferocious animals do not pounce upon it.
Birds of prey do not pounce upon it.
Its bones are frail and its sinews tender, yet its grip is firm.
It does not know as yet the union of male and female;
yet its whole body is full of energy.
This is because its vitality is at its height.
It howls and cries all day long, yet does not become hoarse.
This is because the natural harmony in it is at its height.
To know the natural harmony is to be (one with) the eternal Reality.
To know the eternal Reality is to be illumined.

The whole of the first part of this chapter is devoted to the positive aspects of childhood, when all the existential potential of a human being is not yet actualized, and yet there is innocence and an existential connection to his Origin. These are qualities that most human beings lose when they leave their childhood years behind them and enter adolescence and subsequent stages of life. It is alluding to this fact that Christ said, "Except ye be converted, and become as little children, ye shall not enter into the kingdom of heaven."[72]

In a similar fashion, Lao Tzu compares an individual who possesses virtue with a child. In order to show that a child is innocent and free of sin, he makes several symbolic comments, beginning by saying that a child is immune from being bitten by poisonous snakes. This is a sign that Lao Tzu's words here are symbolic and allegorical, for otherwise they would not be true, since a snake can bite a child just as it can bite an adult.

In a similar manner, Lao Tzu adds that ferocious animals do

72. Matthew, 18:3 KJV.

not attack a child, and here "ferocious animals" can be interpreted to mean false thoughts and corrupt actions. This verse, as well as the following verse, "Birds of prey do not pounce upon it," are symbolic and must not be understood literally. Rather, they indicate that the individual who has preserved within himself the positive attributes of childhood such as truthfulness and innocence will be protected by the spiritual powers of the world of being.

Again alluding to the apparent condition of a child, Lao Tzu speaks of the frailness and fragility of its bones, and then to elaborate on the above symbolism he reminds us that a person with the positive qualities of a child has a firm grip. This denotes the ability to perceive the truth with certainty and steadfastness.

Lao Tzu then states that a child has not yet developed any sexual feelings, yet its body is full of energy. This verse is again symbolic. In the childhood years and the beginning of youth, vitality, and not simply physical strength or speed in walking and running, is at its peak. After this it gradually begins to decline, initially slowly but increasingly more rapidly when one gets older.

Again returning to the specific virtues of childhood, Lao Tzu points out that in contrast to adults, a child can cry and even scream all day without its voice becoming hoarse. This is because a child's being is in the utmost degree of harmony with its nature, and such harmony generally declines with age, with the exception of course of a sage in whose being this harmony always remains. The strange thing is that the knowledge of being in harmony with nature is also essentially present in a child, and this knowledge unites it with the truth. Hence, a child is by nature honest, speaks the truth, and is free from cunning and craftiness.

Finally, Lao Tzu concludes this part by repeating a universal truth: "To know the eternal Reality is to be illumined." Of course, a child is not an illumined sage, but possesses a type of intuitive knowledge, which is itself a type of illumination.

Part II

To try to increase vitality is an ominous act.
The mind squandering its vital health is nothing but an act of violence.
Whatever is too lively and animated becomes soon decrepit.
This is what I would call going against the Tao.
Whatever goes against the Tao will soon come to an end.

One must not try to expend more energy and vitality that exist in one's being. Otherwise, the results will be ominous. One must not foster pointless mental activity and have scattered thoughts. The result of stray thoughts that are always blindly going from one thing to the next will be nothing but violence that harms one's inner peace and tranquility.

The human mind and soul were not created for excessive and aimless activity that does not result in inner peace. If one does not pay attention to this reality, sooner or later one's mind will become exhausted and incapable. This way of living with constant intellectualizing is contrary to the Tao and Its manifestation in one's being.

This part of the chapter ends by mentioning a fundamental truth to which Lao Tzu has alluded previously: whatever is contrary to the Tao will not abide and will soon come to an end.

******

Chapter Fifty-Six

One who knows does not speak; one who speaks does not know.
Block your openings.
Shut your doors.
Blunt your sharpness.
Untangle your knots.
Soften your glare.
Make yourself be at one with dust.
Such I would call the state of mysterious indistinction.
(A man in such a state) cannot be approached intimately.
Nor can one remain distant from him.
One cannot bestow benefit upon him.
Nor can one harm him.
One cannot ennoble him.
Nor can one humiliate him.
Thus, he becomes the noblest of all beings in the world.

The entirety of this chapter provides a description of inner solitude, the withdrawal of attention from the outward, and entering a state of retreat (*khalwah*) in the Sufi sense of the term. The first verse has become a famous Chinese proverb and alludes to the same truth as this well-known Persian poem, which advises avoiding pointless speech:

> Speak rarely and speak choice words, like pearls
> So that from thy speech the world will be filled.[73]

Lao Tzu then tells us to "block the openings," meaning the ways through which one leaves the inner world, so that our attention is focused on our consciousness, the inward, and the truth that is present there. Shutting the doors also alludes to this, and the doors symbolize the outward senses.

"Sharpness" in the following verse does not denote the positive quality of sharpness of intelligence or the power to understand, but rather pointless curiosity and preoccupation with mat-

73. Niẓāmī Ganjawī, ibid.

ters that cause dispersion. As Maḥmūd Shabistarī states,

> He who possesses a reason that seeks that
> which is far-fetched,
> A lot of bewilderment stands before him.[74]

Lao Tzu then advises us to begin to untangle the knots of our soul, which is to say to busy ourselves with inner purification. "Glare" pertains to the outward-seeing eye, so one must see less of the outward, for "the outer eye cannot see that which is hidden."[75]

Next, he tells us to be humble like dust and not to be proud or self-aggrandizing, just as in Persian a humble person is said to be "dust-like" (*khākī*). Attaining these qualities brings one into a state in which the multiplicity of the world of this and that is overcome, or in other words into a state of "indistinction," which, being beyond the comprehension of ordinary people, is named "mysterious." One who has attained such a station of gnosis is exceedingly rare. One cannot approach him as one does ordinary people, yet at the same time he has a power that attracts, as a result of which one cannot remain distant from him.

A gnostic (*'ārif*) has reached a stage in the realm of existence in which he is not in need of anything and one cannot give anything to him. At the same time, his condition is such that nothing can be taken away from him and nothing can harm him. His greatness is such that one cannot ennoble him, and yet he cannot be criticized or humiliated. As a result, such a person is the most precious and the noblest of all beings, and is on a level of existence beyond praise and humiliation.

******

---

74. Maḥmūd Shabastarī, op. cit.
کسی کو عقل دور اندیش دارد   بسی درماندگی در پیش دارد
75. Nāṣir Khusraw, ibid.

Chapter Fifty-Seven

Part I

A state may well be governed by rectitude,
And war may well be won by tactics.
But the whole world is gained only by non-action.
How do I know that is so?
By the following observations:
The more restrictions and prohibitions there are in the world,
the poorer will the people become.
The more elaborate instruments the people possess,
the more confused will the land become.
The more skills and crafts the people have,
the more bizarre will be the objects produced.
The more laws and regulations are promulgated,
the more thieves and robbers will there be.

The *Tao Te Ching* does not deny ordinary positive qualities and some of their uses, and hence it states that it may well be the case that a state may be governed through honesty and rectitude. It is also very possible to win a war by resorting to the right tactics. However, all these victories are partial and transient. The world is gained through another way, not by the way of action but by the way of non-action, in the sense previously described in the text.

The reader may desire further instruction as to how Lao Tzu reached such a conclusion and came to know this truth, and hence he invites us to read the rest of this chapter, before going on to make a series of Taoist observations about the affairs of the world.

From a Taoist point of view, the more restrictions and pressure the government places on the life of its people, the more their condition deteriorates and the poorer they become. The next verse also speaks about man-made instruments and points to an important social reality that is not limited to Chinese society alone. In human history, whenever new tools and devices have been invented life has become more complicated. In the modern world, transformation in the production and use of technology has been growing exponentially. This has resulted in the extremely complicated life of today, in which the decline not only of society but also the natural order is increasing daily.

It is as though Lao Tzu composed these verses pertaining to new inventions and technology for contemporary man. We live in a world in which hardly a day goes by without bizarre new devices being created, marketed and coming to affect people's daily lives. By the time people become accustomed to new inventions, they change, and new tools and machines are created and imposed on people in the name of progress, the negative effects of whose tools are becoming apparent despite their having certain benefits. The net result of this process is the ever-increasing decline of the serenity and inner peace of most people.

Finally, Lao Tzu states that however much rules and regulations increase in society, the number of people who find a way to violate them and resort to some form of theft also increases, and their knowledge of how to violate the law also increases, as has been said,

> When a thief comes in with a lamp on a dark night,
> he will steal more selectively.[76]

Part II

Hence the sage says:
"I remain in non-action, and the people are transformed of themselves.
"I enjoy quietude and the people become righteous of themselves.
"I do not meddle with anything, and the people become prosperous of themselves.
"I remain free from desires, and the people become of themselves like the uncarved block of wood."

In this part, Lao Tzu presents the words of a sage, expressing his attitude to the realities described above. The sage states that, while he remains in his station of "non-action" (*wu wei*), he is not engaged in action in the ordinary sense of the term, and yet the condition of the people will change in a positive way, brought about by the presence of the sage among people without him performing any action.

---

76. Sanā'ī Ghaznawī, *Dīwān*, ed. Mudarris-Riḍawī, Intishārāt-i Sanā'ī, Tehran, 1362/1983, p. 55.
چو علم آموختی از حرص آنگه ترس کاندر شب　　چو دزدی با چراغ آید گزیده‌تر برد کالا

While the sage enjoys stillness, peace and silence, the light of his being shines forth, and as a result of the blessing of that light the people engage in righteous deeds, since they are better able to perceive the truth. Like physical light, the light of gnosis appears to be static and unmoving, yet it illuminates its surroundings.

In this way, the sage does not interfere in the affairs of others through outward action, yet his very presence guides people to felicity and success. Since the sage has gained freedom from the desires of the carnal soul, he becomes an example for people so that they, too, can become like the "uncarved block of wood," and return to their primordial nature.

******

Chapter Fifty-Eight

Part I

When the manner of government is obscure and loose,
the people remain simple and naïve.
When the manner of government is sharp and alert,
the people become endlessly dissatisfied.
Misfortune is what good fortune rests upon.
Good fortune is what misfortune lurks in.
Who knows the limit?
There seems to be no fixed norm.
What is (considered) just turns unjust.
What is (considered) good turns evil.
Indeed, man has long been in perplexity (about this).

As long as a government is not autocratic and oppressive and is "obscure," meaning that it does not oversee everything carefully and grants freedom to people in most matters, people will remain simple and naïve, meaning that they are neither shrewd and cunning, nor compelled to pursue their interests by being crafty and dishonest. However, by contrast, if the government is aware of everything and oversees and interferes in all matters, people will be dissatisfied. To understand the truth of this perspective, it is sufficient for people in our own times to observe their surroundings.

After discussing these two topics, which have political and social dimensions, Lao Tzu returns to considering truths regarding man himself and not society as a whole. Here he states that the foundation of fortune rests on misfortune. The misfortune here is not that of others; rather it is a question of contrasts. If one has never experienced misfortune, how could he know that the positive state he is experiencing is good fortune? This statement is a repetition of the metaphysical principle that was alluded to before, and which in our [Islamic] philosophy is mentioned in the famous verse of Shabastarī, "The appearance of all things is through their opposite."[77]

The complement of this principle is also true. If one were always happy, one would not be aware of one's happiness. This awareness occurs when one loses one's happiness and becomes miserable. It is only then that one realizes the value of happiness. To know the value of a blessing without losing it is not possible for everyone. Most people appreciate the value of their health when they have lost it, and such loss always lies in wait. Thus, Lao Tzu asks, "Who knows the limit?" meaning the limit between happiness and misery, fortune and misfortune, and is aware of his happiness in contrast to misery. Likewise, who knows the limits of everything and acts accordingly such that his fortune will not turn into misfortune and he will remain aware of the line that separates them?

Lao Tzu then alludes to a problem in this matter: it seems there is no fixed norm to resolve this. While certain general principles can be identified, one cannot present a set of instructions that provides specific details that will be useful for everyone. The fact that there is no fixed norm here is one of the most important challenges of human life.

To demonstrate this truth, Lao Tzu presents several examples. The fact that, often in life, what one considers just becomes unjust is something that many people experience on a daily basis. Similarly, what one judges to be good becomes evil. What is intended in this verse is not the truth of principles but rather their application.

This ambiguity in judgment, decision-making and action has always accompanied man and perplexed him, just as in Sufism this world is referred to as the "temple of perplexity" (*dayr-i taḥayyur*).

> O God! In this temple of perplexity I am poor
> but have a heart full [of love].[78]

Part II

Therefore, the sage is square but does not cut things.
He has corners but does not hurt others.
He is straight but does not stretch others.
He is illumined but does not dazzle others.

---

77. Maḥmūd Shabastarī, op. cit.

78. Farīd al-Dīn ʿAṭṭār, *Asrār-nāmah*, ed. Shafīʿī-Kadkanī, Intishārāt-i Sukhan, Tehran, 1388/2009, p. 230.

خدایا من در این دیر تحیر چو آن پیرم تهی دست و دلی پر

The sage's being "square" alludes to his discipline, steadfastness and firmness without him necessarily making use of this firmness. A sage has "corners," meaning a certain fixity and inflexibility. He sees the truth, speaks the truth, and acts correctly, yet he does not put pressure on or "stretch" others. He, in whose being wisdom has come to dwell, does not make pretenses to this in order to dazzle others and attract their attention.

******

Chapter Fifty-Nine

In ruling men and serving Heaven, nothing is better than frugality.
Just by being frugal, one may be said to conform oneself (to the Tao)
from the very beginning.
By conforming oneself (to the Tao) from the very beginning,
one may be said to double and re-double the Virtue.
By doubling and re-doubling the Virtue,
there will be nothing one cannot overcome.
If there is nothing one cannot overcome,
the limit of one's power will be unknowable.
He whose limit of power is unknowable will be fit
to maintain a kingdom.
He who is in possession of the "Mother" of a kingdom
will be able to endure long.
This is what I would call having deep roots and firm stems.
This is a way to longevity and unblinking gaze.

"Serving Heaven" is a Taoist term that, in addition to its obvious meaning of religiosity, has been interpreted in some commentaries as signifying attention to physical, intellectual, and spiritual health, because life is a divine gift. Thus, in attending to one's health and vitality one is serving Heaven, or to use Islamic language, one's Creator and Origin. Frugality in this verse alludes to avoiding wasting of one's physical, intellectual, and spiritual power or using them in vain. Frugality in the sense mentioned, and not only with regard to material things with the goal of gaining more of them, is so important that it can itself harmonize human life with Tao. Taoist spirituality always involves opposition to wastefulness and considers excess to be harmful. This principle applies to all domains, from painting to Taoist ethics.

If from the beginning of one's life as an individual possessing the power of discernment one can be in harmony with the Tao, the virtue one possesses will not only double but will increase many times over. With the assistance of the Tao, not only does virtue grow exponentially, but also no obstacle or force can overcome it or prevent this process of increase from continuing.

When there is no obstacle that can overcome virtue there is no longer any conceivable limit for the virtuous individual's power. It is such an individual, the limits of whose power cannot be known, who deserves to govern the kingdom. The governance of the one who possesses the virtue of frugality in its universal meaning as mentioned above will be stable and will endure for a long time.

Lao Tzu calls the awareness of these realities "having deep roots and firm stems," meaning to be strong and firm in principles (*aṣl*) and their applications (*far'*). He adds that following this path results in longevity and an "unblinking gaze," which alludes to a common practice in ancient China for the preservation of health.

******

Chapter Sixty

Governing a large state is like cooking small fish.
When one rules the world in accordance with the Tao,
the spirits will not manifest their potencies.
Not that the spirits are not endowed with potencies,
but that their supernatural powers do not harm men.
Indeed, if neither of them does any harm,
the virtues will converge into one another.

When one is cooking a small fish, it should not be turned over in the frying pan, which is to say the action of cooking should be accomplished without action. This allusion indicates that a large kingdom should be governed according to the principle of "non-action" (*wu wei*). "Spirits" here refers to beings that are called *manes*, which according to philosophical teachings are alive after death and can influence human life, resulting in ominous or catastrophic consequences. If the king rules in accordance with the teachings of Taoism, the power of these living spirits will not be manifested.

To avoid misunderstanding, Lao Tzu mentions that the non-action of these spirits does not mean that they lack power. Rather, they do indeed possess supernatural powers, but these powers will not harm human beings. Thus, one's mind should be at peace that these spirits will not afflict him.

This truth also applies to the sage. He never harms people, and negative actions do not issue from him. As a result, the people will benefit from the sage, the ruler and the spirits, and consequently the world will enjoy peace and harmony.

******

Chapter Sixty-One

A great state is a low lying land.
It is the convergent place of all the streams of the world.
It is the Female of the whole world.
The Female always overcomes the Male by keeping quiet.
Being quiet, she takes the lower position.
Hence, by taking the lower position, a great state annexes a small state, while a small state, by taking the lower position, becomes annexed to a great state.
Thus, some by taking the lower position annex others,
while others by taking the lower position become annexed.
What a great state wants is only to comprise within it
(as many) men as possible.
What a small state wants is only to be embraced by the other and serve.
Each of the two obtains in this way what it wants.
But it is more appropriate for the great one to take
the lower position.

From a geographical and geological point of view, cities are usually built at the feet of mountains and within valleys, even in mountainous countries, even though there may be some small villages at high altitude. This fact can be seen in two very different countries, namely Afghanistan and Switzerland. However, the meaning of this verse is not limited to its application on the physical plane.

The term "lower position" here denotes receptivity. Natural blessings such as water and wind flow from the mountains to the plains and bestow the fresh air and water necessary for life on the lower areas. Such a lower position is where streams flowing from different directions converge. Here the word "world" does not of course denote the entire world, but rather near and far regions that are connected to the land in question.

Everything that exists in the domain of life is born from the feminine principle, which, like water, is the source of life. In the same way that the Quran states, "And We made every living thing from water."[79] Lao Tzu calls water "the Female [principle] of the whole world."

Presenting the symbol of procreation, Lao Tzu then states that in this act, which is the cause of the continuation of life and the creation of new living beings, the feminine principle is apparently calm. Without mentioning that the masculine principle is active, he points out that it is by the calmness of the feminine principle that it dominates over the masculine principle. That is, it brings about a transformation in the masculine principle resulting in the formation of the first phase of life of a new being in the form of an embryo in the womb of the feminine principle.

By way of allusion, the text then returns to the symbolic, and yet also physical, significance of the lower position, which, by being calm and "keeping quiet" has more effect. From this biological discussion a political conclusion is reached. Instead of trying to gain a higher position, a powerful state can annex a smaller state to its territories by occupying a lower position, which is to say without using violence or aggression. Correspondingly, by occupying a lower position the smaller state is annexed to the larger state and becomes a part of it. The result of this analysis is that by taking a lower position some can annex others to themselves, and others can become annexed by the same means.

Lao Tzu then alludes to the obvious truth that a great and strong state wishes to encompass more people within itself. In contrast, a small state needs shelter and thus is willing to be under the protection of a great power and serve it. If such an arrangement comes about, both the large state and the small one achieve their objectives. With the repetition of these pieces of advice an important conclusion can be drawn: instead of aggression and the use of force it is more worthy of a stronger state to occupy the lower position in the Taoist sense of the term.

******

79. Quran 21:30.

Chapter Sixty-Two

Part I

The Tao is the ultimate depth of the Ten Thousand Things.
It is the treasure of good men.
It is also the refuge of those who are not good.
Beautiful words issuing from the Tao when offered
in the marketplace sell well.
Noble deeds (issuing from the Tao) elevate a man above others.
But (from the standpoint of the Tao) there is no reason
why a man who is not good should be (simply) abandoned.

This chapter begins with a principle that was also previously alluded to in the *Tao Te Ching*, namely that the Tao is the "ultimate depth," meaning the principle of the existence, of all existing things, or to use the terms of the Abrahamic traditions, God is the Creator of the world of existence. Since reality is thus, the Tao is the treasure of good people. Naturally, if one believes in the Origin, this Truth will be his greatest treasure.

However, since the Origin is the source of all existence, not only is It the refuge for good people, but It is also the refuge of those people who have no goodness, whether they like it or not.

Words that issue from the Tao or have their source in the Tao are essentially beautiful, for beauty is one of the attributes of the Divine Truth. When such words are presented even to ordinary people or spread in the bazaar they will be accepted.

Likewise, noble actions and deeds that are rooted in the reality of the Tao grant eminence to man and elevate him in the eyes of others.

Finally, Lao Tzu mentions that, from a spiritual point of view or from the standpoint of the Tao, one must even attend to the one who is not good, and one must not abandon them or leave them alone.

Part II

Thus, when the emperor is enthroned and the three highest ministers are installed, rather than sending to them a large jade disc

followed by a team of four horses, one should remain seated and still and simply present to them the Tao.
Why did the ancients so highly value the Tao?
Is it not because one can thereby obtain what one wants
and even escape the consequences of sins?
Therefore, It has become the most valuable thing in the whole world.

In this part Lao Tzu returns to the domain of politics, making reference to a Chinese tradition in which during the coronation of an emperor, when the three foremost ministers are appointed, a large jade disc and four horses are given to them. Lao Tzu adds that instead of doing this, it would be better to be silent and only bestow on them the Tao, meaning knowledge and true virtue.

After giving this advice, in order to clarify this matter Lao Tzu asks why the Tao was so highly valued in the ancient Chinese tradition. He answers this question with another question: Is it not because if one gains the Tao, one can obtain anything one wishes without any negative consequences? As it is said in Persian, "Be with God and do as you wish."[80] The result of this philosophical and moral teaching is that there is nothing in this world more valuable than the Tao.

******

80. A well-known Persian proverb:
با خدا باش و پادشاهی کن   بی خدا باش هرچه خواهی کن

Chapter Sixty-Three

Part I

Do by not doing.
Be concerned solely with not being concerned.
Find taste in what is tasteless.
Regard the small as great and the few as many.
Requite with good those who have done you wrong.
Plan to deal with what is difficult while it is still easy.
Undertake what is big while it is still small.
All the difficult things in the world originate in what is easy.
All big things in the world originate in what is small.
Hence, the sage never undertakes great things.
Therefore, he ends by accomplishing great things.

This part is entirely devoted to a Taoist explanation of the ordinary actions and reactions of life in a way that is apparently the opposite of how one who does not take recourse to Tao thinks and acts. It begins with that which man always accomplishes, which is to say action itself, advising briefly but profoundly to accomplish action without accomplishing action. This is precisely the principle of "non-action" or *wu wei*, which has been discussed several times previously. Throughout this part, the addressee is not the ordinary individual but the sage. He advises such an individual to concern himself with not being concerned with this or that and to attach himself to not being attached to everything, though of course indirectly implying the words "except the Tao."

The sense of taste in the next verse is a metaphor for delimitation, and Lao Tzu advises his addressee to find the taste of that which is beyond the delimitation of taste. This is another way of expressing the importance of freedom from "anything that takes the color of attachment."[81] A sage must not become attached to those things to which ordinary people feel attached.

In this world, that which is outwardly small and insignificant

81. Ḥāfiẓ, op. cit., p. 27.

in quantity is often great, inwardly and in terms of quality. Hence, Lao Tzu states that one must look into the depths of things and not simply outward appearance and see the great in the small and the few in the many. In terms of its inner meaning, this advice is connected to the Islamic teaching that God is the Rich and His servants are the poor,[82] and seeing the small as great is also an allusion to the spiritual significance of poverty.

Doing good to those who wrong us is among the most fundamental ethical teachings of many religions, including Christianity and Islam. It is also a foundational principle in Chinese philosophy and religion, and is one of most universal ethical and spiritual teachings of authentic religions.

Lao Tzu continues his advice to the sage by stating that before a situation becomes difficult it must be taken care of. In many matters, an issue comes up that is easy to resolve at first, yet most people have a tendency not to deal with it until the small problem becomes a big one, in which case it is often insoluble. The sage must not adopt this approach and succumb to the misjudgment that since an issue is small and resolving it easy, that there is no need to address it.

The following verse completes the previous verse, stating that it is proper for the sage to resolve problems when they are small rather than waiting until they become great. This of course also applies to the upbringing of children and to other creatures. While children are young, one must take care of their upbringing and especially their education rather than waiting for them to grow up. This rule applies to all the living things that surround us as well, from the shrubs one plants in the garden to the cats and dogs one takes care of.

Lao Tzu then gives a reason for what he has said, that the great problems of this world, or at least most of them, start from something small and then grow. This truth is quite noticeable in daily life in the social, political, and economic domains. In this world everything big begins with something small, whether it be the phases of human life or the establishment of social, economic, or political institutions. For example, most large-scale political movements in history began with a few individuals of like mind and then grew from there. Of course, it is also the case that in this world some

82. Quran 35:15: "O mankind! You are needful of God; and He is the Self-Sufficient, the Praised."

يَا أَيُّهَا النَّاسُ أَنتُمُ الْفُقَرَاء إِلَى اللَّهِ واللَّهُ هو الْغَنِيُّ الْحَمِيدُ

things decrease and become smaller, but here Lao Tzu's intention is to bring our attention to the fact that things that are great today were small yesterday.

Then, in a Taoist manner Lao Tzu concludes that the sage does not begin with great steps. He avoids ambition and grandiosity. As the Persian proverbs goes, "He who picks up a big rock does not intend to throw it."[83]

Part II

He who makes easy promises rarely keeps his word.
He who considers many things easy meets with many difficulties.
Therefore, there are many things which even the sage treats as difficult.
That is why in the end he meets with no difficulties.

In traditional civilizations such as the Islamic and Iranian, people's promises were certain and reliable, as many large transactions were conducted based on oral agreements and promises, and this is still true to some extent. This attitude toward promises was also prevalent in traditional Chinese civilization. It is in view of this reality that Lao Tzu states that the value of a promise must be appreciated and one must not make promises easily, that is, without considering the various aspects of a situation and one's ability to fulfill the promise. He who makes a promise without being certain of his ability to fulfill it is necessarily rarely able to follow through.

One should never take the issues one is faced with lightly and must always consider the degree of difficulty or ease of each. Taking all things lightly and without considering their various dimensions will only result in facing many unexpected problems. This is so common in human life that few people can claim never to have experienced it.

In contrast to ordinary people, the sage first examines the details of each issue and realizes that there are things that are difficult to accomplish even for him as a sage, and then acts on the basis of this awareness. As a result, in the end the sage does not encounter problems and is always aware of the limits of his abilities.

******

83. Corresponding to an English proverb, "Barking dogs seldom bite."
سنگ بزرگ علامت نزدن است.

Chapter Sixty-Four

Part I

It is easy to hold anything while it is still stable.
It is easy to deal with anything before its symptoms begin to appear.
It is easy to dissolve anything while it is still soft and fragile.
It is easy to disperse anything while it is still minute.
Deal with anything before it comes into being.
Put anything in order before it falls into disorder.
A huge tree of an arm's span grows from a sprout as thin as a hair.
A nine-story tower rises from a heap of earth.
A journey of a thousand miles begins from the very spot
under your feet.

The verses of this part include a series of pieces of advice that are both applicable in daily life and contains an inner meaning that is particularly useful for one who possesses wisdom. The nature of this world is to be in a constant state of becoming (*ṣayrūrat*), but it is often the case that something at first seems stable and then starts flowing and transforming. Thus, it is better to deal with matters before they enter a state of flux so that one can influence this process of transformation in a positive manner.

There is always a condition that precedes the appearance of the symptoms [of a problem], and Lao Tzu advises that it is better to deal with any issue before these symptoms begin to appear. This is in fact another way of expressing the advice given in the previous verse.

To clarify the truth mentioned above, Lao Tzu presents the following example: it is easy to dissolve something when it is still soft, whereas when it hardens and becomes firm, dissolving it becomes more difficult. This principle is true not only of physical objects but also of intellectual matters. In the same way, so long as something is small, dividing it up and scattering it is easy, and this too is true not only of external, material objects, but also of intellectual and ethical issues.

"Com[ing] into being" in the verse that follows alludes to delimitation and actualization in a coherent manner. It is better to deal with an issue before it reaches that point, rather than waiting until it becomes too late to affect it in a positive way.

Change and the process of becoming (*ṣayrūrat*) often lead to disorder. Thus, Lao Tzu advises us to put things in order before they reach this stage. To clarify this advice, he presents several examples, beginning with the life of a huge tree, which begins as a thin sprout. At that early stage one can change the direction of its growth, but once it grows into a large tree there is no way to do so, because by this time the trunk has taken its final form. Of course, one can cut down the tree or a storm may uproot it, but the general shape of its growth cannot be changed except for fresh branches that have not taken yet their final form. Obviously, this example is based on the natural course of the growth of a tree, since it is of course possible to use various techniques to change the direction of the growth of a large tree, at least to some extent.

> Whoever is not taught the rules of etiquette (*adab*)
> in childhood,
> Will not be saved when he grows up,
> You may turn a tree in any direction when it is a sapling,
> Otherwise, it can be straightened only by fire.[84]

A nine-story building is like a great tree. Just as a tree starts its life as a sprout, a tall building is at first no more than a heap of earth on which all kinds of buildings could be built. However, once a particular building is constructed, its original foundation cannot be changed.

The final example that Lao Tzu presents has become one of the most famous Chinese proverbs and is now used in other languages. No matter how long a journey is, as is alluded to by the words "a thousand miles," it begins with the first step, and that step must necessarily be taken from where one is standing. This principle is obvious in the corporal realm of existence, but its inner meaning may not be so clear. For any intellectual direction that one chooses to pursue or any spiritual path one wishes to follow, one must start from where one is at that moment and not imagine that one can start from where one is not.

---

84. Sa'dī, *Kulīyyāt*, edited by 'Abbas Iqbal Āshtiyanī, Tehran: 1372/1992, *Gulistān*, 7, p. 248.

هر که در خردی اش ادب نکنند　　در بزرگی فلاح از او برخاست
چوب تر را چنان که خواهی پیچ　　نشود خشک جز به آتش راست

In the material world man has no choice but to start his journey from where he stands, but in the realms of thought and spirituality, there is always a potential illusion of seeing oneself in a position or station that is not his and of trying to begin the journey from there. The depth of this verse, which has led it to become a famous proverb is in this symbolic meaning and not in reference to ordinary travel in physical space.

Part II

Whoever attempts to do anything will end by damaging it.
Whoever sticks to a thing will end by losing it.
The sage does not attempt to do anything.
Therefore, he damages nothing.
He sticks to nothing.
Therefore, he loses nothing.

This part contains a few verses that refer back to the principle of "non-action" or *wu wei,* which is one of the pillars of Taoist doctrine. Here Lao Tzu states that if one wishes to *do something*, that is, to intervene in the natural course of events, he will ruin it, which is to say he will remove it from its natural course.

Any attempt to safeguard one's attachment to something will eventually result in losing it, while, by contrast, a sage is always free from "anything that takes the color of attachment."[85] [As the Quran affirms,] "Sovereignty belongs to God";[86] everything is ultimately attached to God, as our sages have reminded us time and again. Anything to which one feels attached is in fact on loan to him, and a spiritual man never forgets who its true owner is.

If a sage does not make effort to accomplish anything it is because of the principle of *wu wei.* He affects his environment by his being and presence rather than by acting upon the beings that surround him. The result of this "non-action" is that there is nothing in the world of becoming that can harm him. Since he has traversed the way of detachment, the outside world cannot affect his spirit or soul or stick to them. As such, the sage never loses anything. He feels no attachment to anything such that he would lose anything when it ceases to exist.

85. Ḥāfiẓ, *Dīwān,* ibid.

86. Quran 40:16: "Whose is the sovereignty this Day? It is God's, the One, the Paramount."

لِّمَنِ ٱلْمُلْكُ ٱلْيَوْمَ لِلَّهِ ٱلْوَٰحِدِ ٱلْقَهَّارِ

Part III

In any enterprise the ordinary people ruin the matter
when they are just on the verge of completion.
Exercise caution toward the end as much as at the beginning
and you will never damage your affair.
Therefore, the sage desires not to desire.
He does not value goods that are hard to obtain.
He learns not to learn.
He thereby returns back constantly to what the common people pass by.
Thus, he assists the spontaneous being of the Ten Thousand Things.
He refrains from interfering with it with his own action.

Many people exert effort while carrying out a task, but before finishing it they consider it complete, stop paying attention to it, and turn to something else. As such, Lao Tzu advises that every task must be pursued until the end so that one's initial efforts should not go to waste and be ruined. His advice is very similar to the famous Persian proverb, "Who is it who has done the work? The one who completed it."[87]

Lao Tzu continues by advising that just as you start any task with utmost care and precision, you should continue showing this precision until the end so that your action will not cause harm. This is an important life-lesson for everyone. In the Islamic tradition there are numerous supplications in which it is asked of God Most High to bring about a good ending for any particular task. But man too has a responsibility to continue to exert true effort and care until each task is complete.

The ultimate desire of a sage is to reach a stage in which he no longer desires. He desires not to desire, to be content with what is and not to seek more. This advice is similar to the response of Bāyazīd Basṭāmī to the question "What do you want?" (*mā turīd?*), to which he replied, "I want not to want" (*urīdu an lā urīd*).[88]

The sage does not struggle to gain that which is hard to obtain and does not value it, which is to say that he does not approach matters in an overly strict manner and does not waste his inner energy. Since he is a sage, he has realized the Truth and no longer seeks to learn that which is non-essential. As such, his effort is

87. کاررا که کرد؟ آنکه تمام کرد

88. Farid al-Dīn 'Aṭṭār, *Tadhkirat al-awliyā'*, Tehran, 1375/1996, Chapter 14.
أُريدُ ان لا أُريد

centered on learning not to learn things that are unnecessary and potentially misleading. Ordinary people act in a manner contrary to this, and thus the sage returns to the foundations and principles of things, to which ordinary people pay no attention.

This knowledge of the sage is instrumental in the actualization and moment-by-moment manifestation of the beings of this world. This takes place even without any intervention on the part of the sage or any effort to influence the natural course of the manifestation of beings and their lives.

******

Chapter Sixty-Five

From of old, those who excel in the practice of the Tao do not have recourse to It to enlighten people with knowledge, but rather to bring them to non-knowing.
If the people are difficult to govern,
it is because they have too much knowledge.
Thus, he who rules the state by means of knowledge damages the state.
He who does not rule by means of knowledge brings prosperity to the state.
To know these two (principles) is the standard measure (of the ruler).
And to know the standard measure in every matter is what
I would call a mysterious virtue.
Mysterious virtue is deep and far-reaching.
At first glance, it seems to work contrary to the nature of things.
Yet, in the long run it turns to great conformity.

If one examines the verses of this chapter considering their outward meaning, they may seem to contradict the truth; yet their inward content is otherwise. Here Lao Tzu states that it has always been the case that when sages, who are experienced in practicing the Tao, want to enlighten ordinary people on the path of knowledge, they do not apply the Tao. Rather, they guide them to a state of unknowing. Here "knowledge" denotes unnecessary information and knowledge of unnecessary details, and not true gnosis (*ma'rifat*). To attain true gnosis one must purify the tablet of the spirit of unnecessary knowledge with the help of the Tao, as is said [by Rūmī]:

> The tablet of the Sufi is not knowledge and words,
> It is nothing but a pure heart white as snow.[89]

This principle also applies to governing the people, since the more ordinary people accumulate inauthentic information, the more difficult governing them becomes.

The result of these principles is that if the state is governed only on the basis of considering outward knowledge and material needs, the state will suffer. Thus, one must govern the state by ap-

89. Rūmī, *Mathnawī*, II:159.

plying principles rooted in wisdom and not just by paying attention to outward affairs. By contrast, though this sentence is only implied, if a ruler does not rule by way of outward knowledge and the resulting lack of attention to the reality of things, he will make his kingdom prosperous and happy.

Lao Tzu considers the two principles mentioned in these verses to be the criteria of the correct actions of a ruler's governance. In contrast to the "knowledge" mentioned at the beginning of this chapter, Lao Tzu considers knowledge of these criteria to be extremely valuable, and names it "mysterious virtue." This praiseworthy quality named "mysterious virtue," which was also mentioned previously, is a very profound matter, and as a result deeply influences the lives of the people. On the surface and from the point of view of one who only sees the outward aspect of things, it may seem that this mysterious virtue is contrary to the nature of things. However, this is not true; the mysterious virtue ultimately results in widespread harmony within human life itself and in our relationships with nature and all other beings.

******

Chapter Sixty-Six

The reason why the great River and the Sea can be the king of the Hundred Valleys is that they are content with occupying the lower position. So, they become the king of the Hundred Valleys.
On (the basis of) this principle, if one wishes to rule over the people,
one must lower oneself to them by using humble words.
If one wishes to be in front of the people,
one must keep oneself behind them.
In this way the sage takes his place above the people;
yet, they do not feel his weight.
He takes his place in front of the people; yet,
they do not consider him a hindrance.
Therefore, the whole world finds pleasure in supporting him,
and never becomes weary of him.
He does not contend with anybody.
Therefore, nobody in the world is able to contend with him.

Many commentators consider "the great River" to refer to the Yangtze River in China, but it can also be considered to refer to any great river. Both the River and the Sea are positioned lower than the land around them, which is why Lao Tzu makes use of them allegorically in this verse. The River and the Sea spatially occupy a lower position, and for this very reason rule over all the valleys and meadows around them like a king, since they provide them with water and thus make life in them possible. All this is possible because of the River and the Sea occupying the lower position. To emphasize this truth, Lao Tzu repeats that it is for this reason that they are "the king of the Hundred Valleys."

Lao Tzu draws a political and social lesson from this analogy, stating that, in a similar manner, if one wishes to govern a society, meaning of course in a way that is successful from a Taoist point of view, one must like water take up a low position, which is to say, one must act and speak with humility. Taoist sages' criticism of most governments originates from this idea, for most rulers lack the virtue of humility.

According to this same teaching, if one wishes to become a leader of the people, one must not stand in from of them, but rather take up a position behind them. One must lead without claiming leadership. By following this path, the sage maintains his position above ordinary people, yet the people will not perceive his leadership and guidance and therefore will not act contrary to his teachings. Under such circumstances everyone will be happy to support him, will be content with his rule, and will not tire of it.

One of the most important truths is that such a ruler does not contend or compete with anyone, and hence there is no one who can contend with him. Naturally, competition is something that requires two parties to exist.

******

Chapter Sixty-Seven

Everybody under Heaven says the Tao I uphold is certainly vast
but appears stupid.
Yea, It appears stupid because It is vast.
If It were clever and smart, It would have diminished long ago.
I have three Treasures, which I hold firm and cherish.
The first is mercy.
The second is frugality.
The third is not daring to stand at the head of the world.
Being merciful, I can be courageous. Being frugal, I can be generous.
Not daring to stand at the head of the world, I can be the head
of all able men.
If one tries to be generous without being merciful, if one tries to be generous without being frugal, and if one tries to stand at the head of the world without keeping oneself in the rear, the result will be nothing but death.
He who fights out of mercy will win the battle,
and a country defended with mercy will remain impregnable.
Heaven itself, when it wills to save something, guards it with mercy.

This chapter begins with an extraordinary verse, which states that all people agree that my path, i.e., that of Lao Tzu, namely the Tao, is certainly vast, even though It appears foolish to ignorant people. Indeed, if true gnosis (*ma'rifat*) does not appear foolish to the ignorant, then it is not true gnosis, since ignorance by its very nature negates knowledge. Since ordinary people cannot recognize the vastness of the Tao or the Way, the Tao appears foolish to them. If cleverness were the characteristic of the Tao, it would have lost its vastness and disappeared long ago.

Lao Tzu then speaks of three treasures that belong to him and that he cherishes and holds firmly. The first treasure, which is inseparable from the Tao, is mercy, which as the Quran also states, "encompasses all things."[90] This mercy is never separate from the

90. Quran 7:156: "My Mercy encompasses all things."
وَ رَحْمَتِي وَسِعَتْ كُلَّ شَيْءٍ

Absolute Truth, and for this reason in the Islamic tradition every act is begun with the Name of God, accompanied by the Attributes of Compassion and Mercy, using the phrase "In the name of God, the Compassionate, the Merciful."[91]

The second treasure is the quality of frugality, which is not simply material but applies to all actions and results in observing the appropriate boundaries and limits in every matter.

Lao Tzu's third treasure is the absence of daring and audacity for attaining status and the refusal to take up a position at the head of this world in the outward sense.

Each of these three treasures is accompanied by a specific virtue. If one can be merciful, he can also be courageous. If one is frugal, he can also be generous. If one does not have the audacity to take a place at the head of the world (using violence and conflict), he has the capacity to become the leader of society.

By contrast, if someone wishes to attain his objectives without possessing the requisite virtues, which is to say to show himself to be courageous without being merciful, to be generous without being frugal, or to use effort to stand at the head of worldly matters instead of setting himself behind the people, the result with be nothing but destruction and death.

In contrast to this, Lao Tzu reminds us that if someone engages in conflict out of mercy and not to amass wealth and power, he will be victorious. If he defends his country on the basis of mercy and not merely on force, that country will be impregnable and invincible. The fundamental reason for this truth is that if the Tao, the celestial Truth, Itself wishes to protect something, It does so out of mercy.

******

91. بِسْمِ اللهِ الرَّحْمنِ الرَّحِيم

Chapter Sixty-Eight

An excellent warrior does not use violence.
An excellent fighter does not lose himself in anger.
He who excels in defeating his enemy does not treat the enemy as an enemy.
He who excels in employing men humbles himself before them.
This is what I would call the virtue of non-contending.
This is what I would call making the best use of the ability of others.
This is what I would call being in conformity with Heaven.
This was the supreme Principle of the ancients.

This chapter presents the highest example of Taoist concept of the true warrior. For those who are familiar with early Islamic history, it is as if in presenting this description Lao Tzu had 'Alī ibn Abī Ṭālib in mind. The founder of the Taoist tradition states that a superior warrior does not act with violence. Rather, he enters the battlefield with sincerity and truth in view, distanced from personal anger, [as Rūmī states] "Learn sincerity in action from 'Alī."[92] An excellent warrior is in control of his carnal soul and does

92. Rūmi described 'Alī's encounter with 'Amr ibn 'Abd Wadd in the Battle of the Ditch (*khandaq*). 'Alī's behavior set an example and revealed his qualities and station and defined spiritual chivalry forever in Islamic history. See, *Mathnawī*, I:167f.:

Learn sincerity in action from 'Alī,
Know that the Lion of God was purified from deception.
In a battle he vanquished an exemplary knight
Quickly he drew his sword [to kill him]
His enemy spat on 'Alī's face,
What a face! The honor of all prophets and Friends of God
At the moment 'Alī threw his sword away
And refused to kill such a lowly enemy,
The man wondered why 'Alī did not kill him as he could, he asked,
What was the reason for such an untimely forgiving? Answered 'Alī,
I wield my sword for the sake of the Truth,
I am His slave, not the slave of my body,
I am the Lion of God, not the lion of my passion,
My action gives testimony to my faith,
I do not desire, but what He wills,

not allow his anger towards his enemy to cause him to lose this control, even if his adversary does not act in this way and treats him with anger, [as described by Rūmī] even if the enemy spat on Alī's face who was the pride of every prophet and Friend of God.

This is because the true warrior is the servant of the Truth, not of his body and carnal soul.

Indeed, [as Ḥāfiẓ states], "The comfort of this world and the next is hidden in two phrases; being chivalrous with friends and tolerant with foes."[93]

Such a hero (*pahlawān*), who embodies the ethical qualities of the warrior, does not treat his opponents as enemies even while holding the upper hand over them. This is because he wields his sword on the path of the Truth and not for the sake of his personal desires and goals. As a result, his opposition to his enemies is not personal; on the individual level, he does not hold anger toward anyone. His opposition is to corruption, falsehood and whatever is against the truth, and not toward any individual.

This virtue is also applicable to success in employing others. A wise individual does not act toward those he employs with violence and oppression, but rather is always humble toward them. Lao Tzu calls this praiseworthy quality "the virtue of non-contending." That is to say, an excellent warrior does not contend with others, or in common terms is not always looking to pick a fight. In the traditional civilizations of the Far East, this virtue was particularly emphasized among the Samurai of Japan, as can be seen in many descriptions of their lifestyle. This method, rather than bullying and exerting pressure, is in fact the best way to make use of the capabilities and talents of others. This way of acting is also in conformity with the spiritual principles that govern human life, and thus is in harmony with the spiritual and

---

No love but the love of the One is in my heart.

از علی آموز اخلاص عمل　　شیر حق را دان مطهر از دغل
در غزا بر پهلوانی دست یافت　　زود شمشیری بر آورد و شتافت
او خدو انداخت در روی علی　　افتخار هر نبی و هر ولی
درزمان انداخت شمشیرآن علی　　کرد او اندر غزااش کاهلی
گشت حیران آن مبارززین عمل　　وز نمودن عفو و رحمت بی‌محل
گفت من تیغ از پی حق می‌زنم　　بندهٔ حقم نه مامور تنم
شیر حقم نیستم شیرهوا　　فعل من بر دین من باشد گوا
جز به باد او نجنبد میل من　　نیست جز عشق احد سرخیل من

93. Ḥāfiẓ, op. cit., p. 5.

inner reality of man and the Truth of Heaven.

At the end of this chapter, Lao Tzu reminds us that everything he has explained about proper conduct was considered the supreme Principle by the ancients and hence has been observed since time immemorial.

******

Chapter Sixty-Nine

Among the strategists there is a saying:
"I do not assume the aggressive but stand on the defensive.
"Rather than advancing one inch, I retreat one foot."
This is what is meant by the sayings:
"Marching without marching.
"Rolling up the sleeve without showing the arm.
"Seizing the enemy without seizing.
"Grasping weapons without grasping."
There is no calamity greater than underestimating the enemy.
By underestimating one's enemy, one will surely lose one's own treasure.
Thus it is that when two armies raise arms against each other,
the one that fights in sorrow wins the battle.

This chapter continues the discussion of the Taoist perspective on being a warrior from the previous chapter and begins with a saying of the strategists, who represent this ideal type of warrior. This saying begins with words uttered by a true warrior, who recalls that he never takes an aggressive position in battle, but instead adopts a defensive one. Here it is important to note that in the Islamic legal tradition, although some Sunni scholars have considered offensive war to be legitimate in certain circumstances, Shi'i jurists consider only defensive war to be legitimate and in accordance with the Sharī'ah.[94] Since it is defensive military action that is under consideration here, the warrior states that in battle he does not advance an inch, but rather retreats a foot for every inch he might move forward. Sages in the centuries following Lao Tzu wrote many well-known books on the art of the proper conduct of war in which they discussed these issues.

Since such statements may seem strange, in the verses that follow Lao Tzu describes the true warrior in his own words. The outward actions of a true warrior may give the impression that he is marching, but in fact he is not marching, which is to say that he

94. On the Shi'i position on war, see Mohammad H. Faghfoory, *Ethics of War and Peace in Islam: A Shi'a View*, Chicago: ABC International, 2019.

has not taken a step toward victory. He rolls up his sleeves, meaning that he prepares to act, without showing that he is doing this or "showing the arm." He overcomes his enemy and captures him without outwardly having done so. He takes up arms to fight without having outwardly taken up arms.

After these statements presented in the voice of the true warrior, Lao Tzu continues in his own words, stating that to underestimate the enemy is a great catastrophe. This piece of advice is repeated frequently in Islamic texts, as in Sa'dī's *Gulistān* (*The Rose Garden*),

> Do you know what Zāl said to Rustam the Champion?
> "One must never underestimate an enemy!"[95]

The Noble Quran itself guides man in this way, warning him not to underestimate an enemy, and particularly Satan, who is his greatest enemy.[96]

Alluding to the same truth, Lao Tzu adds that underestimating the enemy and considering him weak will undoubtedly result in one losing his treasure and whatever is of value for him. He concludes that when two armies meet each other in battle, the one that fights "in sorrow" will succeed. In this verse, "sorrow" does not carry its contemporary psychological meaning. Rather, it denotes a spiritual state that includes an absence of grandiosity and exaggeration of one's strength and a lack of desire for revenge or pleasure in obliterating the enemy.

******

95. Sa'dī, *Kulliyāt-i Sa'dī*, ed. Muḥammad 'Alī Furūghī, 1320/1941, p. 19.
دانی که چه گفت زال با رستم گرد؟ دشمن نتوان حقیر و بیچاره شمرد

96. See for example, Quran 2:168: "O mankind! Eat of what is lawful and good on the earth, and follow not the footsteps of Satan. Truly he is a manifest enemy unto you," and 36:60: "Did I not enjoin upon you, O Children of Adam, that you not worship Satan – truly he is a manifest enemy unto you."
يا أَيُّهَا النَّاسُ ... لا تَتَّبِعُوا خُطُوَاتِ الشَّيْطَانِ إِنَّهُ لَكُمْ عَدُوٌّ مُبِينٌ
أَنْ لا تَعْبُدُوا الشَّيْطانَ إِنَّهُ لَكُمْ عَدُوٌّ مُبِينٌ

Chapter Seventy

My words are very easy to understand and very easy to practice.
Yet, no one under Heaven understands them
and no one puts them into practice.
My words come out of a profound source,
and my deeds come out of a firm principle.
Yet, no one understands it; therefore no one understands me.
Those who do understand me are rare.
That precisely is the proof that I am precious.
The sage, indeed, wears clothes of coarse cloth,
but carries within precious jade.

The first-person singular pronoun in this chapter refers of course to Lao Tzu himself. The message of all prophets has an outward meaning that is for everyone and an inward meaning that is addressed to the select few (*khawaṣṣ*). The *Tao Te Ching* is not exempt from this rule, for as the Quran states, "With hardship there is ease."[97] Thus Lao Tzu states that his words are easy to understand and to act upon. Of course, this does not apply to all the verses of the *Tao Te Ching*. Some verses dealing with metaphysics and the inner journey toward the Truth are both difficult to understand and to practice. Only a sage in the traditional sense of the term is capable of understanding both dimensions and putting them into practice.

It is in light of this truth that he expresses the second verse, which seemingly contradicts the first. Thus he states that despite his teachings being easy, no one, meaning no ordinary people (as opposed to the select few) understands them or puts them into practice. This is a complaint that we also see in the statements of other prophets.

Lao Tzu then reminds us that his words are not superficial but rather originate from a profound source, and that his actions are not simply outward activities, but rather manifest from the firm

97. Quran 94:4-5:

إِنَّ مَعَ الْعُسْرِ يُسْرًا فَإِنَّ مَعَ الْعُسْرِ يُسْرًا

principle of the Truth and indeed from Being Itself.

Lao Tzu complains, as have other leaders of religions, that ordinary people do not understand his message and thus do not understand him. However, he also indicates that this does not apply to the select few (*khawāṣṣ*). Since their numbers are always few in comparison to ordinary and ignorant people, those who understand him, although they exist, are rare.

The fact that those who understand Lao Tzu's teachings are few proves that he, meaning Lao Tzu, is precious. The awareness of the manifestation of the Truth encompasses all beings, if one pays attention to things in their deepest reality (*kunh*). Since this matter is not understood by everyone, one is rare indeed who is aware of the inner reality of things, who witnesses the manifestation of the Real and True, who recognizes It, and who knows that "Everywhere there is, there are the rays of the Face of the Beloved."[98]

Like Sufis who wore rough garments made of wool, Taoist sages usually clothed themselves in coarse cloth. Yet under these outer clothes they carried within themselves precious jade.

******

98. Ḥāfiẓ, op. cit., p. 44.

Chapter Seventy-One

He who knows yet behaves as if he did not know is the highest.
He who does not know yet behaves as if he knew is defective.
It is by knowing a defect to be a defect that one can be defectless.
The sage is defectless because he is aware of his defect as a defect.

He who acquires true knowledge and is wise in the Taoist sense of the term does not make pretentions to knowledge and avoids boasting that he possesses knowledge. Such an individual has the highest status among people. By contrast, he who lacks knowledge but makes claims to possessing knowledge is defective. [As it is said]:

He who does not know, and does not know that [he] does not know,
Will eternally remain in compound ignorance.[99]

In order to become free of defect one must first recognize one's defects in order to overcome them. One cannot free oneself of defects without first knowing oneself. In Islamic philosophy also, self-knowledge is considered a condition for knowing God, as the famous Persian saying goes, "Know yourself in order to know God,"[100] as also the motto of the Socratic school, "Know thyself!"

A sage is one who has recognized his defects as defects and thus has set out to remove them. As a result, he has become defectless. Removing defects is impossible without knowledge of human defects. First this knowledge is necessary and then action in accordance with it.

---

99. This poem is attributed to Amīr Fakhr al-Dīn Maḥmūd ibn Yamīn (685/1286-748/1368).

آنکس که نداند ونداند که نداند   در جهل مرکب ابدالدهر بماند

100. This statement is mentioned as a ḥadīth in some classical Sufi and literary sources. However, many early scholars including Zarkashī, Suyūṭī, Ibn Taymīyah and others reject the idea and attribute it to Yaḥyā ibn Mu'ādh Razi (d. 258/872) a Sufi master and contemporary of Bāyazīd. He spent his youth in Balkh and then went to Nayshābūr where he died and was buried. He was a master preacher hence the epithet Wā'iẓ. See 'Attār, *Tadhkirat al-awliyā'*, op. cit., pp. 426-444.

Chapter Seventy-Two

If the people lack the sense of awe for the Awesome,
awful punishment will descend upon them.
(One who has the sense of awe for the Awesome) does not consider
his dwelling place too narrow.
Nor does he dislike his own livelihood.
He does not detest anything; so he is not detested by anything.
It is for this reason that the sage, knowing himself,
does not display himself; loving himself does not exalt himself.
Verily, he rejects this and chooses that.

Awe and bewilderment (*ḥayrat*) have a mystical meaning beyond their ordinary meaning, as the Prophet reportedly said, "O Lord, increase us in bewilderment of Thee!"[101] God's Greatness and Majesty as well as His Beauty and Mercy bring one who is aware to the station of spiritual bewilderment, upsetting and destroying the ordinary limitations of the mind, thought, and imagination, and leading the sage to a state of spiritual intoxication. It is in reference to this state of intoxicating bewilderment that Ḥāfiẓ wrote,

The possessors of "intellect" are the pivotal point
of the compass of existence
But love knows that they are wandering
in this circle in bewilderment.[102]

He who does not experience bewilderment before that Supreme Reality is truly deaf and blind to the realities of existence and therefore will experience awful punishment. The denial of the Divine Reality cannot but have profound negative effects on the soul of the denier. By contrast, he who is in a constant state of perplexity and awe before that Sublime Reality, which is truly Awesome and bewildering by Its very Essence, is unconcerned with the limi-

101. رَبِناَ زِدْنِا تحيّراً" فيك

102. Ḥāfiẓ, op. cit., p. 131. Translation by Seyyed Hossein Nasr, in, *Knowledge and the Sacred*, Albany: State University of New York Press, 1989, p. 315.

عاقلان نکته پرگار وجودند ولی   عشق داند که در این دایره سرگردانند

tations of the outward and physical aspects of his life. No matter how limited his dwelling may be from a quantitative point of view, it would not be narrow for him or cause him to feel restricted, for while he is outwardly dwelling in this limited space, his spirit is journeying in the limitless heaven of the celestial world.

Similarly, he is not discontented with his profession and means of livelihood even though he may not find it to be in harmony with his nature and inclinations, for he does not find the satisfaction of his soul in his work and profession; rather, his goal is to live with the Tao.

A sage does not hate anything on the plane of ordinary life of the world (though by nature he hates the rejection of spiritual teachings). Since he does not show hatred toward others, they also do not feel hatred toward him, however much their perspectives may differ.

In the daily life of ordinary people, hatred is often accompanied by a feeling of grandiosity and pride, but this is not the case for the sage. He is aware of the preciousness of the treasure of gnosis that he carries within himself, though he is never pretentious and boastful about it. He loves the spiritual substance within him, but never tries to show himself as great, and his words, deeds, and comportment are always intertwined with humility and modesty. Thus, the sage distances himself from all self-conceit and grandiosity and instead chooses lack of pretense and humility.

******

Chapter Seventy-Three

He who is bold in being reckless will be killed.
He who is bold in not being reckless will stay alive.
Of these two (attitudes) one is beneficial and the other harmful.
But who really knows what Heaven hates?
Therefore, even the sage finds it difficult to decide.
It is the way of Heaven not to contend, and yet to overcome; not to speak and yet to respond correctly; not to summon and yet let things come of their own accord; to be slack and slow and yet plan well.
The net of Heaven has wide meshes.
They are wide, and yet nothing slips through them.

Boldness can be a positive trait when it is a sign of courage, but recklessness is a blameworthy characteristic that is incompatible with virtue, and also with traditional manners in a general sense. A reckless individual, as a result of a certain type of arrogance, tries to transgress his own limits and be more than he is. As a result, he will face his own destruction and "be killed," which in this verse can be interpreted literally or according to its inner meaning, indicating the destruction of his spiritual substance.

By contrast, since boldness is not in itself a negative trait, if someone is bold and courageous but not reckless, he will be saved from destruction and death. Lao Tzu concludes that being bold without being reckless is a positive characteristic, while boldness accompanied by recklessness is a harmful quality. The third verse is thus simply the logical conclusion of the first two verses of this chapter.

However, despite this explanation, making a judgment on this matter is difficult and thus Lao Tzu asks, What is it that the Heaven truly hates?; and since the focus of his attention is man, we can also say "Who is it that Heaven hates?" This subtle ethical point has always preoccupied the attention of sages and gnostics, [as Farīd al-Dīn 'Aṭṭār] said,

> Among us who knows who the truly pious person is,
> [Who knows] who is saved and who is wretched?[103]

Judgment regarding this subtle point is so difficult that even for a sage it is not easy to reach a conclusion.

After explaining this important point, Lao Tzu returns to discussing the Way of Heaven, which is manifested in the very being of a true sage. The Way of Heaven is that one does not contend in the Taoist sense of this term and yet attains victory. A sage whose being is intertwined with the Way of Heaven does not speak, yet responds correctly to everything. He does not summon others [to himself], but allows them to come to him by their own volition. In everything he does, such a sage is slow and contemplative, yet everything is planned well in advance. Although this verse concerns a sage most of all, in the traditional world it is possible that the Way of Heaven also manifest in other forms, such as through fairies (*parī*) and jinn, and not only through human beings.

In various traditions, the Message of Heaven is sometimes likened to a net by means of which fish, indicating the people living in this sea of becoming, are caught and thus saved from becoming. This symbolism is used in the last verses of this chapter, which also adds that the meshes of this net are wide, and thus encompass a vast expanse of reality. However, despite the width of these meshes, no beings escape them. This is the assurance that religion or the Way of Heaven gives to its followers.

******

103. Farīd al-Dīn ʿAṭṭār, *Asrār-nāmah*, op. cit., p. 231.
که داند تا به معنی متقّی کیست   سعید از ما کدامست و شقّی کیست؟

Chapter Seventy-Four

When the people are no longer afraid of death,
how can one frighten them with death?
If on the contrary people are always afraid of death, and the ruler is able to arrest and put to death those who do evil, then who would dare (to do evil)?
There is, however, a real Executioner charged with the task of killing.
To kill in place of the Executioner may be compared
to someone cutting wood in place of the master carpenter.
In cutting wood in place of the master carpenter,
few can escape hurting their own hands.

Commentators often interpret the first verse of this chapter as expressing the state of people who, as a result of a corrupt and oppressive government, have become distraught, sorrowful and desperate, seeing no possible solution for their situation. As a result they no longer fear death, and thus can no longer be governed by frightening them and threatening them with death, for such threats will not be effective. However, this verse also has a spiritual meaning. A true gnostic and sage who has experienced voluntary death before his physical death is no longer afraid of death.

Even in dire situations, the reactions of all people to their situation will not be the same. Some will still fear death and surrender to the situation no matter how unpleasant it may be. Since the ruler can arrest them and even kill those who commit serious crimes, people no longer rebel and commit crimes because they do not dare to do so. Lao Tzu is thus alluding to the universal rule that the people *can* be brought under control and governed using fear, and this universal rule has been observed in most periods of history throughout the world and continues to be so today. This lack of daring is thus a significant obstruction to the people committing unworthy and corrupt actions.

After discussing these important social issues, Lao Tzu then turns to an important metaphysical and also religious principle. He reminds us that there is an Executioner who is charged with the task of killing. That which Lao Tzu calls the real Executioner is the Tao Itself, though in Its negative and destructive aspect, and this point contains a universal metaphysical principle. In the Hindu tradition, Brahma is the creator and Vishnu is the preserver, while Shiva is the destroyer of creation. Similarly, in Islam God is both the Giver of Life (*al-Muḥyī*) and the Bringer of Death (*al-Mumīt*). He is the Source of Mercy but also of Justice, and He causes everything to return to Him.[104]

In Chinese philosophy, the Tao both gives existence to "the Ten Thousand Things" and returns them to the state of non-being in the Taoist sense of the term. It is this latter aspect of the Tao that is referred to as the universal and real Executioner. However, this power belongs to Tao alone and not to other beings, who must not resort to killing (except of course in self-defense). If someone wishes to engage in the destruction and killing of other people like the Tao, he is like someone who has no knowledge of the craft of carpentry and yet cuts wood in place of the master carpenter. The result of this is that the work will be ruined.

Continuing the analogy of the carpenter, Lao Tzu concludes that if some people wish to carry out the work of a carpenter without the necessary knowledge and experience, only a limited and exceptional group of them will escape injuring their own hands. As it is said,

> Not every goat is capable of threshing.
> It demands the experience of an old man
> and the strength of a bull.[105]

******

---

104. See Quran 2:28: "How can you disbelieve in God, seeing that you were dead and He gave you life; then He causes you to die; then He gives you life; then unto Him shall you be returned?," 10:56: "He gives life and causes death, and unto Him shall you be returned," and 50:43: "Truly We give life and We cause death, and unto Us is the journey's end."

وَكُنْتُمْ أَمْوَاتًا فَأَحْيَاكُمْ ۖ ثُمَّ يُمِيتُكُمْ ثُمَّ يُحْيِيكُمْ ثُمَّ إِلَيْهِ تُرْجَعُونَ
هُوَ يُحْيِي وَيُمِيتُ وَإِلَيْهِ تُرْجَعُونَ
إِنَّا نَحْنُ نُحْيِي وَنُمِيتُ وَإِلَيْنَا الْمَصِيرُ

105. The English equivalent of this proverb is, "Big boots do not fit every man."
کار هر بز نیست خرمن کوفتن گاو نر میخواهد و پیر کهن

Chapter Seventy-Five

If the people are hungry, it is because the ruler taxes them too heavily.
Therefore, the people are hungry.
If the people are difficult to govern, it is because the ruler meddles too much with their affairs.
Therefore, the people are difficult to govern.
If the people make little of death, it is because the ruler is too eager in his pursuit of life.
Therefore, the people make little of death.
Indeed, he who lives without striving after life is wiser than the man who values life too highly.

In traditional Chinese society the central government was much stronger than in other parts of the world and collected regular taxes from the people. When the people's economic condition was poor, the payment of these heavy taxes naturally resulted in the poverty and thus the hunger of the people. Lao Tzu emphasizes that it is precisely these excessive taxes that cause the people's hunger.

From the Taoist point of view, the main faults of government result from excessive interference in people's affairs. As Lao Tzu mentioned previously, the less the government interferes in people's lives, the better. A government's difficulties with the people originate from its excessive intervention in their affairs. In these verses, Lao Tzu explicitly repeats this teaching several times: the excessive intervention of the government in people's lives is the cause of the difficulties of governing society.

If people are pushed to desperation and life loses its meaning for them, death loses its significance and they may even welcome it. If this happens and people are no longer afraid of death and consider it insignificant, it is because the ruler or the ruling class pursue their own interests and are concerned with their own lives beyond what is reasonable and with too much eagerness.

Lao Tzu then repeats that in such circumstances the people will be under such pressure that death will appear insignificant.

The truth of the matter is that one who passes his life without exerting excessive effort to meet his needs is wiser and more intelligent than one who values his daily life (not his spiritual life) such that he spends all his energy and effort in fulfilling his daily needs.

******

Chapter Seventy-Six

Man at his birth is tender and weak, but when dead, he is hard and stiff.
And so are the Ten Thousand Things.
Grass and trees are tender and fragile while alive, but once dead,
they are dry and stiff.
Thus, the hard and stiff are the companions of death.
The tender and weak are companions of life.
Thus, an army which is too powerful is liable to lose the battle.
A tree which is too strong is liable to break.
The strong and big end by being cast down, whereas the tender
and weak end by occupying higher places.

Everyone knows that when a baby is born its skin is soft and it is weak and helpless. Yet after death the body of the same person will become hard and stiff because life has been taken away from it. This truth also applies to all of "the Ten Thousand Things." All plants, from grasses to trees have a kind of softness and fragility so long as they are alive. Yet when they die, they lose their softness and become brittle and dry, as in Persian, a dead plant is said to have "dried out."

Presenting these examples, Lao Tzu concludes that the attributes of brittleness and rigidity belong to the realm of death and dead things, while by contrast softness and weakness, in the sense of lacking the strength and resistance to pressure that a dead piece of wood has, are characteristic of living beings. Of course, this analogy is only relative, as a living being can also accept a certain amount of pressure and remain alive.

From these principles Lao Tzu draws a practical lesson, explaining that an army that is too strong and thus lacks flexibility may be defeated in battle for this very reason, since it has the power of a dead piece of wood in resisting pressure but lacks the flexibility of a branch of a living tree. He adds that a very strong tree may break in a strong wind, and what is implied in this verse is that the weak branches of the tree may bend in the same strong wind but will then return to their original position.

The final conclusion of this discourse is that whatever is big and strong (from a physical rather than a spiritual point of view) will eventually break and fall to the ground, whereas that which is seemingly weak and soft will survive. In the human realm, one with these characteristics will attain a high position in society since he possesses the quality of "non-action."

******

Chapter Seventy-Seven

The Way of Heaven may be compared to the stringing of a bow.
The highest part is pressed down.
The lowest part is raised up.
That which is excessive is removed.
That which is insufficient is supplied.
Thus, the Way of Heaven is to take from what is in excess
and supply what is deficient.
Otherwise is the way of man.
It consists in taking from those who are in want and giving it
to those who have in excess.
Is there anyone who, having himself things in excess,
is ready to offer them to the whole world?
Only he who embodies the Tao.
Therefore, the sage accomplishes his task, yet does not boast of it.
He accomplishes his task, yet does not stick to his own merit.
Is this not because he does not wish to display his superiority
over others?

Since the use of the bow and arrow was very common in ancient China, frequent allusions to them are found in Chinese philosophical texts. The first verses of this chapter provide an example of this type of allusion. As such, Lao Tzu states that the Way of Heaven, or that which is in harmony with the Tao, "may be compared to the stringing of a bow." To string a bow, one must apply pressure in order to bring its highest part down and its lowest part up. By doing so, the excess length of the unstringed bow is removed, and that the qualities of the bow that do not suit the process of stringing are brought under control. Lao Tzu uses this symbolism to illustrate the Way of Heaven in so far as it removes that which is in excess and gives it to that which is lacking, compensating for the deficiency.

The way of ordinary human beings is different from this and in fact is contrary to it. It is to take from those who are in need and to give what is taken to those who are not in need and have more than enough.

Then Lao Tzu asks: In the world of ordinary people, is there anyone who has possessions in excess and yet is willing to offer those excess possessions to all people? The answer to this key question is that only he who takes recourse to and embodies the Tao is capable of doing so. Such an individual is a sage who accomplishes his actions according to Taoist principles without having a sense of grandiosity or being boastful.

The function of the sage is to perform his duties without becoming arrogant or relying on the ability and merit of his individual soul, much like the idea of living according to one's *dharma* in Hinduism.

Finally Lao Tzu asks: Is it not by virtue of his awareness of the Tao and his acting in accordance with It that the sage has no interest in revealing and boasting of his superiority as a sage? It is evident that here the awareness of the Tao is considered the foundation of correct action, despite this truth being presented in the form of a question.

******

Chapter Seventy-Eight

There is in the world nothing softer and weaker than water.
Yet, in attacking things hard and strong nothing can surpass it.
Indeed, there is nothing that can take its place.
The weak overcomes the strong.
The soft overcomes the hard.
Everyone in the world knows this;
yet no one is able to put this into practice.
Therefore, the sage says:
"He who assumes upon himself the filth of the state is really worthy to be the ruler of the state.
"He who takes upon himself all the calamities of the state is really worthy to be called the king of the whole world."
Words of truth often sound paradoxical.

In previous chapters of the *Tao Te Ching*, Lao Tzu has alluded to the symbolism of water many times. In this chapter, he returns to this symbolism, reminding us that there is nothing in this world more subtle, softer and seemingly weaker than water. Despite this quality, nothing is superior to water in attacking and dominating hard and strong things. Nothing else can replace water in this and do what water can do. Completely embodying the Taoist point of view, he concludes that, in contrast to what one might suppose, it is ultimately the weak that will dominate the strong. Similarly, that which is soft will eventually overcome that which is hard. This is a self-evident truth that everyone knows. However, there is no one (except a sage) who can act in accordance with this truth. It is in view of this truth that a sage says: he who accepts all the negative aspects of governance like water, which dissolves all filth and impurity within itself, has the right to govern the state. And he who accepts all the difficulties and afflictions of governance deserves to be considered the king of the entire world.

Since accepting this truth is not easy, Lao Tzu adds that such words are often difficult to believe, for a statement that contains the truth often contradicts that which the majority of the people believe to be true.

Chapter Seventy-Nine

When a deep-rooted rancor is pacified, some resentment is bound to remain.
How can this be considered good?
Therefore, the sage, holding the left-hand tally, exacts no payment from the other.
Men of virtue know how to deal with tallies.
Men of no virtue know only how to exact payment.
The Way of Heaven has no favoritism.
It is always on the side of good men.

Even if hostilities are old and deeply rooted, it may still be possible to transform them into peace and friendship. But even though wise people have said 'why not free ourselves from rancor?',[106] in most cases it is likely that some degree of resentment will nevertheless remain and it is difficult to be free of this completely. Since this is the case, Lao Tzu asks how this can be considered good. By asking this he is indirectly suggesting that it is better not to hold rancor or hostility in the first place.

In Chinese culture, the creditor holds on to the left-hand side of the tally [in which the debt is recorded]. When a sage loans money, in contrast to ordinary people he does not ask the debtor to repay him. A wise man knows "how to deal with tallies" that are the proof of his transactions, that is, with generosity, forgiving debt, and without pressuring the debtor. By contrast, a man who is unwise or lacks virtue only knows how to ask his debtor for what he owes him. The Way of Heaven or the teaching of the Tao is such that It does not discriminate between people or show favoritism, and, with regard to the rules of the Tao, views all people the same way. At the same time, the Tao or the Way of Heaven

106. This statement is an allusion to Rumi's poem in *Diwān-i Kabīr,* ed. Furūzānfar, no. 1535, p. 257:

Resentments cast darkness on friendships and love.
Why do we not push them out of our hearts?

غرض‌ها تیره دارد دوستی را   غرض‌ها را چرا از دل نرانیم

always takes the side of good over bad and supports those whose deeds are righteous.

******

Chapter Eighty

Just like a small country with a small population,
There are men of great abilities, each being equal to ten or even a hundred men, but they find no place to use their abilities.
The people regard death as no slight matter.
Nor are they induced to move to distant places.
Although there are ships and carts, there is no place for them to go.
Although there are armor and weapons, there are no occasions to display them.
The people are taught to return to the use of knotted cords, find relish in their own food and beauty in their own clothes.
Happy and contented with their own homes, they find delight in their old customs.
The neighboring country is just there within sight.
The cocks' crowing and the dogs' barking in that country can be heard in this country.
Yet, the inhabitants of the two countries grow old and die without ever visiting one another.

This chapter is very well-known among Chinese people, who consider it a description of an ideal Taoist society or a Taoist "utopia," a society that supports tradition and rejects the complication of daily life and that which is today called "progress." As such, it begins by mentioning that which is ideal for human society, namely that a country be smaller rather than larger in size and have a smaller rather than greater population. It is remarkable that such as statement is found in the sacred book of a tradition belonging to one of the most populous human societies throughout history.

In such an ideal society, there are many men of great talent who are the equal of ten or even a hundred men, but since they live in a small society there is no place for their talents to become manifest.

Lao Tzu has previously spoken about death from a spiritual point of view, but here he means that life in the ideal society that he envisions is so good that people do not want life to come to an end. As a result, they do not consider death an insignificant matter. Since they are happy with their lot and life, they see no reason to migrate from their birthplace to faraway lands. They have the means to travel, such as ships and carts, yet there is no place for which they would be willing to leave their homeland.

In their small country, instruments of war such as shields and weapons can be found, but since peace prevails there is no opportunity to use them. In such a country, ancient and traditional skills such as knotting cords[107] will have become popular again, and the people will be taught to enjoy the pleasures of ordinary life such as eating and wearing fine clothes. Since people will be happy in their own homes and satisfied with their lives, they will enjoy preserving ancient traditions, manners and ways of life, and naturally will not be constantly in search of innovation. Since their country is small, the country neighboring them will be so close that they will be able to hear the barking of the neighboring country's dogs and the crowing of their roosters. Yet despite this closeness of the people of these two neighboring countries, they will pass their lives and die without having anything to do with each other or visiting one another.

This entire chapter presents an image that is precisely the opposite of the large urban centers and empires that have ruled over China during various periods of history. It is perhaps because of this contrast that this chapter has attained particular fame in the traditional culture of China.

******

107. An ancient Chinese handicraft dating back to the Tang Dynasty (618-907 C.E.). The artist uses a single piece of rope to create designs with specific forms and auspicious meanings, often used as good-luck charms and decorations. See: https://www.amazon.com/s/ref=dp_byline_sr_book_1?ie=UTF8&field-author=Lydia+Chen&text=Lydia+Chen&sort=relevancerank&search-alias=books. Lydia Chen, *The Complete Book of Chinese Knotting: A Compendium of Techniques and Variations*, North Clarendon, Vermont, 2007.

Chapter Eighty-One

Part I

Truthful words are not beautifully adorned.
Adorned words are not truthful.
He who is really good does not talk much.
He who talks much is not really good.
He who really knows does not display wide knowledge.
He who displays wide knowledge does not really know.

Since the text of the *Tao Te Ching* contains much beauty, the first verse of this chapter seems strange. However, "beautifully adorned" here signifies words used with attention given only to their formal beauty with no consideration of truth, such as when skillful penmanship is used only to show the formal beauty of words without taking into account whether they are true or not. It is nevertheless still the case that the *Tao Te Ching* was and continues to be written in beautiful Chinese calligraphy while at the same time possessing extraordinary spiritual beauty. The Holy Quran is a supreme example of this wedding between truth and beauty of expression, and the spiritual masterpieces of various civilizations, from the *Gulshan-i rāz* (*The Rose Garden of Divine Mysteries*) of Shaykh Maḥmūd Shabistarī and the *Dīwān* of Ḥāfiẓ to Dante's *Divine Comedy* and the *Bhagavad Gita*, also possess this quality.

Again alluding to pretense in the use of language, Lao Tzu states that words adorned with formal beauty yet devoid of inner beauty are not truthful, as is often seen today in a great many works of modern art. The advice that a truly good person speaks little was mentioned in a previous chapter. To speak little but selectively is advice not only found in Persian culture[108] but is also a foundational virtue in Chinese culture and has had a profound effect on Chinese literature. Most Chinese poems are concise, and it is the skill of the poet to express the most meaning in the fewest words and to avoid, as the common phrase has it, beating around

108. Niẓāmī Ganjawī, *Laylī-u Majnūn*, ibid.

the bush. This quality is also seen in Japanese poetry, especially the *Haiku* form.

Lao Tzu again mentions the opposite of this principle, considering the one who speaks much not to be good, since as a result of excessive speech he will express much that is useless and even contrary to the truth. Few people have the knowledge and wisdom to both speak much and to always utter words that are filled with truth and precious like pearls. A rare example of such an individual in Islamic civilization is Rūmī, who spoke much in his works, without this quantity diminishing the sublime quality of his speech.

In a similar way, one who possesses real knowledge does not boast of or make pretenses to being knowledgeable. By contrast, he who claims vast knowledge and boasts of knowing everything, in reality has no share of true knowledge at all.

Part II

The sage does not hoard things.
He uses all he has for the sake of others; yet, he has more and more.
He gives all he has to others; yet, he is ever richer.
The Way of Heaven benefits without doing any harm.
The Way of the sage is to do things without ever contending.

This set of verses, which allude to fundamental truths concerning the wise and the unwise, leads Lao Tzu to return to discussing the characteristics of the sage, an individual possessing real knowledge. Lao Tzu affirms that the sage never seeks to hoard or accumulate material possessions. His state is precisely the opposite of one whose soul is controlled by desire. A sage gives away whatever he has for the sake of others, but in contrast to what may be expected, that which he possesses is always growing. He gives his wealth to others but is always becoming richer. Of course, the quality of richness here is not limited to material possessions, and it can also be said that the spirit of a sage becomes richer as a result of sharing knowledge and ethical teachings. In the Islamic tradition it is taught that the very understanding of the Quranic teaching that God is the Rich and man is poor results in the inner richness of the human spirit.[109]

---

109. Quran 35:15, "O mankind! You are needful of God; and He is the Self-Sufficient, the Praised."

يَا أَيُّهَا النَّاسُ أَنتُمُ الْفُقَرَاءُ إِلَى اللَّهِ ۖ وَاللَّهُ هُوَ الْغَنِيُّ الْحَمِيدُ

The teachings of Taoism, and religious teachings in general, which are precisely "the Way of Heaven," benefit man without harming him. Lao Tzu brings his words to a close with the following truth, that has been repeated throughout the book: the sage follows the path of "acting without acting," meaning that he accomplishes action without struggle and contention, which is to say, by virtue of being who he is.

******

With gratitude to Ercument and Ikbal Tokat
for their generous support of this book.